P9-CQN-608

B
5134
.R3464
B44

Belfrage, Sally,
1936-

Flowers of empti-
ness

FLOWERS OF EMPTINESS

FLOWERS OF EMPTINESS

REFLECTIONS ON AN ASHRAM

Sally Belfrage

THE DIAL PRESS  NEW YORK

Published by
The Dial Press
1 Dag Hammarskjcld Plaza
New York, New York 10017

Manufactured in the United States of America

First printing

Design by Oksana Kushnir

Library of Congress Cataloging in Publication Data

Belfrage, Sally, 1936–
    Flowers of emptiness.
        1.   Rajneesh, Acharya, 1931–   2.   Philosophers—
India—Biography.   3.   Life.   4.   Belfrage, Sally,
1936–   I.   Title.
B5134.R3464B44   291.4   80–25283
ISBN 0–8037–2523–X

The author would like to thank the sponsors of the MacDowell Colony, where this book was written.

For Eve and Moby

FLOWERS OF EMPTINESS

"There is a deadening redundancy to women's writing now," says a poet. There is a deadening redundancy to women's lives, is one answer. A day in my redundant life that began as usual ended with the offer of an encounter with a guru in India. It was the last bit of territory, geographical or spiritual, to occur to me; but I was losing my closest English friends to it, and went tracking that friendship. I found, instead, myself. This was unexpected because (a) I wasn't lost, and (b) I didn't consider that any swami had a roadmap to my soul. I was not only right but wrong on both counts. I found nothing there that wasn't here already, and the guru had no special access to my coordinates but he did help me to see that I did. It isn't what, but how you look at it: a trick of focus. Because the way I looked at it kept changing, I have kept the diary form and present tense here. But there is cheating: Although nothing is related that I did not witness, the exact words of Bhagwan Shree Rajneesh were only available later when they were published by the Rajneesh Foundation.

June 16

Making dinner for the women's liberation group is not the same as any other cooking. Even after eight years together we surpass ourselves for each other. I bought a special roast for last night and splurged on two pounds of cherries, and had a ratatouille half made by the time the children got home from school. But then Jon appeared, stricken with sorrow and needing to talk about the end of his marriage. People always come to me because they know I'm home, but people with newly ended marriages make a special point of it. Maybe they think I know something about the subject. All I know is that it pains me less now that my pain's object, my husband Bernardo, has gone to Portugal and I don't have to see him all the time. But I knew how Jon felt so we opened a bottle of wine and drank it, and by the beginning of the second bottle he was laughing almost as much as he was crying. Unfortunately I forgot about the ratatouille and it burned, forgot to put the meat in on time, and forgot about the cherries, so not until Jon had gone did it occur to me they'd vanished. The stems were located in a dish in the living room.

"Where are the *stones?*" I accused my son, whose mouth was red.

He said he'd swallowed them. I gathered it was a half-hearted effort to destroy the evidence.

"Do you feel all right?"

"I don't know."

I'd just managed to get Moby into the bath when I was almost struck down by the sound of the doorbell ringing on time. How could they come on time? But relief: It was Judith. I'd always rather do anything with Judith around than with Judith not around, even though her state of contained excitement seemed to portend a crisis. She has a way of looking damp and pink, and especially beautiful, when she is agitated, but the outer signs rarely divulge a clue as to whether the condition is positive or negative.

She helped to get the food faintly organized while I confirmed that Moby for some reason felt fine and got him and Eve to bed, and in the smallest of spaces when we could talk before the bell rang again, "What *is* it?" I asked, and Judith blurted out, "Dinah and I have got you a ticket to India."

What?

The world turned around.

How to think of it? DREAM. Why? Are they feeling sorry for me, tired of my moaning about the loss of my children to their father for the holidays? Do they want my company? Maybe they think they can remodel me? Or can it really be just friendship? Does it go so far? To India?

Judith was inscrutable. They were going, she simply shrugged, and wanted me to come too. Simple. We've always done things together, don't want to leave you out. But you can't buy my enthusiasm for what you're doing. Another shrug. They can try?

There was no time to pursue it; the others came. I mechanically fed us while my mind was busy furnishing itself as an Eastern bazaar. I have never felt so rich, so

4

chosen. Judith and her presents! Dinah is the deeply generous one, if only because of her unattachment to things:
she'd as soon give as keep them. But nobody ever had a
more perfect sensitivity for giving, for what is given, for the
occasion, than Judith. It almost makes me want to forgive
them for going to India themselves. If only I weren't so
frightened they'll stay forever. Perhaps it was to ward off
such considerations that she told me about the ticket when I
couldn't comment.

Dinah has already been to Poona twice and become a
"sannyasin" (official convert) of her guru, Bhagwan Shree
Rajneesh: typical outrageous Dinah-type behavior except,
having failed to interest her children in living there with her
despite a six-month experiment, she has now brought them
home to London to their father and is returning to India
without them to stay. To *live*. This desertion goes beyond
outrageousness to outrage as far as I'm concerned, a view
Judith shared to begin with—Dinah's decision to opt out of
motherhood provoked Judith's most scathing psychiatric
prognosis and, in a letter she read to me for support, she
predicted "bins or suicides" for the abandoned twins. The
letter had no effect on the decision, though the row between
Dinah and Judith—who was accused of interfering grossly
and without understanding simply to create guilt—rang out
in my direction for months: in mine, because for a while
they stopped directly communicating. But now from being
an intermediary in their dispute I seem to have become
maternity's standard bearer. Judith, from whom I expected
continuing solidarity, started showing it in quite the other
direction by attending "meditations" at the London
Rajneesh Centre, and lately by preparing an Eastern pilgrimage of her own during her month off from her patients
(whom *she'll* never abandon, she insists, the way Dinah's
done with *her* children; their need is even greater, and be-

sides there are more of them). Even Stuart the lodger is going, either as new sannyasin or lover of Dinah or friend to them both or all three. They have been making me *furious*, and now what a way to call my bluff. Do they really think that I am guru fodder? That I'll approve their latest craze? Do I care? *India!*

But they are being odd. In the note which Dinah, who arrived next, handed me with the actual ticket, they write that I'll need a cholera shot and an orange robe. Why notes when we're all here? And the way they are at dinner, while none of us mentioned it to the others: Dinah's strong thin face with its huge blue eyes is a study in impassivity, though Judith can't suppress a Look now and then. What *are* they up to? They seem to have more in mind for me than a mere easterly plane trip. But surely we've known each other too well too long for them to expect conversions from me—there's nothing to convert. I'm so irreligious that my atheism is apathetic. And if this isn't a religion it's another of their damn therapies: they've gone in for so many and tried to interest me often enough surely to know. . . . I've never joined anything. I don't believe people who claim a solution. I distrust even the possibility of solutions. Guru? It's a four-letter word. About this Bagwash, as Dinah quaintly calls him, I know little except that he won't let beggars in his ashram, which is quite enough to lose me; and he's given Dinah a new name, something outlandish and idiotic, *Ma Prem Pankaja,* which I won't ever call her anyway; and made her wear only orange (in which she looks as *Vogue*-y as ever—it's not by any means the shaven-headed-saffron-Buddhists-of-Oxford-Street sort of thing—Dior or Chloé will do as long as it's orange) and a mala (amulet) around her neck containing a picture of his hairy visage dangling from a bunch of nuts; and above all stolen her from me, not to mention from her children. She doesn't seem any happier. She used to be a productive writer, and she's given that up. It's not as if her orange cohorts have much appeal. The ones I've met are exclusive, fanatic, boring, and beneath her; also familiar in this slavish age. If Bhagwan were Billy Graham, they'd be out crusading; if he were Charles Manson they'd be out killing; if he were Mao they'd be working hard and dressed in blue instead. The sannyasins are inevitably well-off, if only in the posthippy flower-child sense of caring little for cash but always able to summon up enough to fly halfway around the world, and of course to keep the ashram solvent. It's the kind of background money that enables mothers to nip out for a visit on a whim or a worry, as Dinah's mother did. It's also the kind of money that seems to breed in its owners dissatisfactions requiring extreme measures to put right. Through with radical politics, drugs, communal living, feminism, psychoanalysis, encounter groups, they're seeking still more exotic solutions for problems that are luxuries in the first place. Now it's "Who am I?" I think there are better questions, even to lead to the same answers. For most of the world there are *other* questions. But life to many of my friends is becoming a monologue, a process of *finding the self.* How did the self get so lost? Maybe it comes from living in crowds.

Along these lines we quarrel, mock, insult each other—or did. We don't seem to now. I was always thinking: Dinah will be back soon. I was learning to live without her, or not without her so much as with missing her, with the sorrow of her absence. And the constant hope: Dinah will be back soon. When she came, it was only to announce a visit and you could see the balance shifting. I got very angry. But the arguments didn't affect her, the rage never moved her. She was vanishing, like water through a gauze, still visible but out of reach. It was becoming distinctly dreamlike, watching Dinah's pursuit. I used to think I could follow her, but something has got unsynchronized or disconnected, or I'm missing the tools to respond. I think of my little boy forging through an impenetrable mass at a fair shouting back, "Keep track of me!" Or of what R. D. Laing said after his last trip to the States, about people besieging him with the plea, "How can I get in touch with my feelings?"

This strange question occupies Dinah's new friends. I would like to talk to them, but we don't seem to have the words in common. I met a group first at a party Dinah gave before she'd ever gone to India, in honor of some who were leaving next morning. She invited other people too—assuming perhaps that as they all got on inside her head, why shouldn't they outside? But soon the party split into two parties. The sannyasins went into the living room and there was a lot of raucous orange dancing and groping, while the rest of us sat in the kitchen with our drinks and smokes, idly watching them. They didn't like us watching them, idly or not, and closed the door between the adjoining rooms. Somebody on our side got up and opened it again. One on theirs closed it. This went on—among us it became an amusement—until one of them announced quite fiercely that hereafter, the door was to be *shut*. Not much of a party after that. I tried to infiltrate at their end but they weren't interested in groping with me. What seemed particularly strange, though, was that while these people were going to India for the first time in the morning, they weren't curious to meet Jai, an actual live Brahman who was present (at our end). Not one of them gave him a glance. Jai thought they were funny.

I thought they were funny too; but resented, as usual, having to take them seriously even to quarrel with them— to learn more about their ideas than I ever wanted to know if only to take issue. This has always been my grudge against mystics. Most people's enthusiasms don't necessarily leak all over you (films, gardening, East African tribal customs), but mystics claim to have found The Way not just for themselves but for you too, if only you'd recognize it, and how can you discuss it with them when they can rightly dismiss you for ignorance? Of all things, I now find myself reading this monthly newsletter Dinah has sent to me from Poona. Harmless enough: Bhagwan talks of Being Here Now and living totally and the god within us all. Nothing very unusual, though no less acceptable for that—but why forsake your life and wear a uniform? If his advice has any intrinsic value, surely that resides in its application to life, not exile. He's always bashing away at the ego, so presumably no orange person would dream of wondering what it is in Bhagwan then, since it can't be ego, which compels him to surround himself with worshipers. When I ask such questions of Dinah, she usually ends up saying that he doesn't actually exist in the sense that we know it: he is an enlightened master, on a level quite beyond my earthling inquiries.

I felt I understood a little more (though not much) from a novel Dinah was hawking around London on behalf of its sannyasin-author about the latter's history with Bhagwan. I couldn't see from it how the heroine was better off at the end than at the beginning (nor her seven children, from having been reallocated to their various fathers) but the middle certainly kept her busy. She'd simply given herself over. Such an extreme abandonment of responsibility *of* the self in the name of a greater responsibility *to* the self is obviously seductive—there you are, given carte blanche to redo you, be concerned with nothing outside your skin to the end of becoming concerned with nothing inside it, boundless ego-trip to lose the ego—though it nags at me that the appeal is similar to that which encourages sleep in a snowdrift. Do you ever wake up? But the novel's heroine was an abstraction, and Dinah is my friend. If even *Dinah* can be so readily enslaved (it's called "surrender" out there and is much recommended) that she can desert her life and loves and believe a living man is God—for so she does —I find it altogether weird, not to say dangerous. Is my mind closed? Am I just seeking buttresses for my resentment against this fakir for filching my Dinah, and now quite possibly my Judith? (I've already read enough newsletters to know I ought not to put those "mys" in there. In fact, Dinah's children are not even "hers." The trouble is, Felix and Emily are obviously wondering, whose children are they, then?)

As for seeking buttresses, on Dinah's first return to London I certainly collected a few. It wasn't just the beggar story which appalled me but the report that this enlightened master had "finished with sex in his past lives and doesn't need it anymore" and that his was the only air-conditioned house in the ashram. Finished with sex but not with air conditioning? What is that? Because not invented in past lives? And that he emerges from his palatial hideaway, where three young women take care of him, only at dawn before it's too hot and evenings after sunset, while everybody else puts up with his native heat. He isn't old, midforties, but claims to be ill, verging on the terminal, and predicts the early forfeiture of "this body." Photos of him do not bear this out. He could not possibly look more robust. But he is troubled with allergies of all kinds, diabetes, and *asthma*. This interests me, because I've had asthma, enough to know about the crazy subterranean feelings inspiring it. It is not a condition associated with divinity. But clearly the alleged brevity of his current stay on earth breeds urgency among his disciples. Otherwise why not enjoy and take care of your children and then go to India? And this: The human touch (for all its being, evidently, the chief currency among his followers) distresses him, Dinah said, causing him to tremble. *Really*. I ended up feeling: I don't even like this man.

But why be finicky now? It's one thing to develop a prejudiced mythology if you haven't the slightest chance to encounter the facts, but this ticket requires a fresh start. I owe Judith and Dinah that. Maybe that's what it's about. Anyway all these considerations pale beside their extraordinary gesture. The chance to see Bombay! Goa! I'd given up hope that I'd see India. If I have any religion at all it has to do with people, friends capable of such generosity and all our fellow passengers, the hands I'd like to shake. Even Bhagwan's, if it wouldn't make him tremble.

June 17

D irectly from dropping the children at school, I go to collect Judith and Dinah at the London Rajneesh Centre after their morning meditation. I suppose I ought to join in these activities now, but luckily they are all scheduled for times when I'm giving children breakfast or dinner. One of these days.

I stop outside just as they emerge, their arms around each other in deep communion. They don't see me at first, and for a moment I'm so stunned by some current coming from them that I cannot move. Long, strong, great women

—angular, blond Dinah with her wiry boyish body and Virginia Woolf-ish face; younger, darker, taller Judith, softer too, perhaps: until you look at Dinah's eyes. How could life without them be endurable? Who could I call when I'm seething to say something? Who would understand what I meant? Who would comfort me, rejoice, encourage me with my work, *be there*? They *can't* not be there. It can't happen. How long have I been saying that?,

Sitting at our favorite café I tried to find out more about this ticket and the impulse for it. The most they'd say was they "just thought it would be nice" if I came too. Nice? Dinah vaguely thought it had begun, or ended, with Stuart, who, tiring of their conversation on the matter, grumbled, "Oh why don't you just buy her a ticket"—and given their recent concern with worldly goods and their disposal, Dinah reckoned since she has to sell some shares to mend the roof another ticket only costs a fourth of *that*, so why not? But the thing is, she said, looking off edgily, they were awfully apprehensive about my reaction.

"Why?"

"We thought you'd be angry at us."

"What for?"

"For trying to manipulate you."

"Manipulate me?"

"That's how I'd have felt. Once Frank sent me a ticket to New York and I tore it up."

I was much puzzled. Obviously they want to win me round, but the cost of a ticket could hardly influence my feelings, except to make me extremely grateful. "I guess anybody who wants to manipulate me with tickets can go right ahead."

Anyway, while Judith is off to see her psychiatric supervisor to discuss her patients, Dinah and I go shopping for orange clothes. Don't know what I'm doing with this matter of orange. Certainly there's no plan to join them (somehow it is understood Judith will take sannyas) and I'll never go so far as a mala, but it may prove inconvenient to stick out like a clothed person in a nudist colony. Apparently I need some sort of robe to meditate in anyway, but failing to find one end up with two T-shirts, a sun dress, and Dinah's promise to show me to her Poona dressmaker. Shopping is incredibly simplified if you only look at orange. (Or pink-ishy peach to rust; the range is very wide.) The other bonus is how it seems to flatter the wintry gray English complex-ion. It is meant to attract "good vibes," says Dinah, who confessed, "I wore green underpants once last week so I fought all day with Felix." This piece of intelligence was passed on at Marks & Spencer's underwear counter, where a feeble joke about the lengths one was meant to go provoked it as a perfectly serious response. Since my intention is in-conspicuousness merely, the answer is phooey to orange underpants. (In any case I haven't got a private-income mentality and am appalled at the waste. Dinah and Judith, living off inheritance money, are beyond this consideration.)

We called back at the Rajneesh Centre, on the fifth floor of a factory-loft building. It's called Kalptaru—"wish-fulfill-ing tree." Harmoniously, peacefully laid out. After sam-pling some orange lavatory paper, I followed Dinah into a reception room where cubbyholes stuffed with orange robes on two walls are matched by people wearing orange robes on the other two: sitting hunched in a row on the floor resting after, Dinah supposes, a session of "shouting nasty things about their mothers." A big room next door with an expanse of olive carpet (room interiors are supposed to be green to repulse the "good vibes" toward the clothing), huge blowups of Bhagwan's bearded face, windows on three sides, and two couples nesting, one lot drinking tea and the other swooned into a corner, limbs unerotically entangled. I was the only one in the "wrong" color, and those faces acknowledging my presence at all registered a vaguely hostile blankness, as if I'd dived into their tank, a blatantly alien species, and tourist fish were not welcome. As we left I saw a huge heap of shoes by the door, as at a mosque or a Dutch farmhouse. I'd neglected to take mine off. Were those robes in the cubbyholes for use by such as me? I asked—since I'm going to try a meditation on Sunday. But they're apparently for the people doing a "two-week enlightenment intensive." I do wish they wouldn't use that language.

I also wish the trip involved no one but Dinah and Judith and me. The people at the ashram sound as intimidating as the local devotees look. Neil said yesterday, "You do realize don't you that if you're not with them you're against them?" —and I object, I only want to witness, but is that possible without exciting the baddest vibes since green underpants?

On the subject of a friend of his who'd gone to Poona, Neil—an actor/director who is more Sufi-inclined—gave a multimedia demonstration of his understanding of the structure there. Using a matchbox to represent Bhagwan on a cigarette packet meant to be the ashram placed on a newspaper for Poona, he mapped it out as a sort of board game. "You start out here"—he indicated the fringe of the newspaper—"and advance toward the goal, two forward one back sort of thing, and with any luck and the right effort you could just manage to stay at the ashram itself, even live in it for good (or what counts for good out there), getting nearer . . . nearer . . . and the winner gets *right inside*"—the matchbox. "The idea is to come as close as you can to the Big B. All parts merged." He smiled. "On his terms, of course."

June 18

Kissing Eve goodnight, I told her that while she's in Portugal I'm going to "Dinah's place in India." I've never talked to her on the subject, but she's overheard me often enough to know about Dinah and her children. Now she shot straight up in bed demanding, "Are you going to see *that man?*"

"What man?" as if I didn't know.

"That man Dinah thinks is God."

"I should think so. I hope so."

"You're not going to get hypnotized, are you?"

"Don't worry. I'm not the type."

"Do you promise?" I've never seen her so intense in her nine years.

"I promise."

June 19

Talking to my old friend Mary last night about my various misgivings, I realized there is a calmer (and perhaps less offensive to sannyasins) perspective from which to see it. She said she has found in her work as a builder and joiner in a male world a set of views and a spectrum of behavior so bizarre that she hardly knows any more if gravity exists, and is compelled to believe that rational thought is not an adequate instrument for interpreting experience. She doesn't know what that instrument is, but of the Bhagwanites—at least "they're on to the same thing" and such efforts deserve attention. The search for "more productive ways of thinking." I don't really know what she's talking about, but unlike the others she makes me want to know.

I was reminded today of something else she'd said when I passed a group of half a dozen robed and turbaned Englishmen—members of a local Sufi sect—parading, as one, down my street. Mary and I had been talking of the orange question. "I should think," she observed, "that people in uniform are less, not more, able to find out who they are as individuals." (But are they supposed to find out who they are as individuals?)

June 20

Irst meditation. At Judith's little house (where all three—Judith, Dinah, and Stuart—are living) to pick up anyone else going too. Find Judith engrossed in a migraine acquired at another early-morning meditation (Dinah suffers some indeterminate ailment from them too, and won't go anymore), leading me to wonder if, like the homeopathic "cure" for smoking I underwent a couple of years ago, it "works" by making you so horribly ill that mere reversion to normal (achieved by the cessation of treatment) represents recovery. Since I feel perfectly well, I am in no mood to be tampered with. Judith assures me however that ghastliness is to be expected. I refrained from mentioning that, should this prove the case with me, I shall leave them to it.

Dinah and Stuart appeared and volunteered to accompany me and perhaps even join in, since this is just "the humming meditation, awfully tame, for new people." Indeed the Centre this time contained many non-oranges (a glimpse into the meditation room revealed two naked peachy colored men—does that count?). Poonam, a distracted looking woman with flaming orange hair and freckles, explained the procedure to the novices. "For half an hour," she said, "you all hum. Close your eyes or get a blindfold. Try to think of yourself as a hollow tube. You can hum any way you like but there's no need to make a tune of it. Try to keep your back straight. Then a gong goes off I think and you do this"—and before I can wonder about that curious *I think* I'm caught up in a demonstration of a palms-up, out-sweeping gesture which we're all meant to copy—"for seven and a half minutes. Then for seven and a half more minutes you turn your palms down and do the opposite."

Someone asks, "Why?"

"The first is to get rid of bad energy," explained Poonam, "the second to welcome new energy. Then another gong and it is quiet for fifteen minutes. You may lie down then if you like. Twenty-five p. please and fifty if you're staying for the lecture" (a tape of Bhagwan).

Paying up I heard an astonished voice call my name, and there was an extremely orange old acquaintance called Liz, reintroducing herself as "Anatta," late worshiper at other thrones, among them the smoke-cure homeopathist who made me so ill. She's been a sannyasin for a year, she said, and "I've heard constantly about this 'Pankaja,' but my god I never realized it was *Dinah*."

In the large meditation room they drew the curtains and about twenty people collected sweaty orange blindfolds from a cache on the side and arranged themselves with pillows (cheating, leaning on the wall), while Poonam put on the tape and slid out the door, closing it behind her. Very odd reverberating gonging noises: could be either primitive or electronic. Hummmmmmmm. Inhale. Hummmmmmmm. Terrible urge to sneeze; no handkerchief. Were you allowed to get up to fetch some orange lavatory paper? Can't hum with clogged nose. What a failure I am. Now here comes the sneeze. Measures are necessary: forget it or will it away. Hmmmmmmmm. Well, that's done. Now what? How boring. I thought of some Bhagwanian books I'd picked out beforehand, excessively expensive, and how much more illuminating they might be than this. Hmmmmmm. Have a look at the others. Just a little peek. Edge up blindfold, squint one eye. Aha. I spy another doubter, someone in the corner peeking too. Others dead serious, shutters down, nostrils flared. What to think about? "Try to think of yourself as a hollow tube." As thoughts go, it's not very satisfactory. How about This too will pass, a remark someone not long ago actually attributed to Bhagwan. Look at him, smirking at me poster-size from every wall and pillar. Why do they all insist he's so "beautiful"? Perfectly ordinary bearded bald chap, seems to me. Looks a bit like Bernardo if anyone. Oh shut up, try harder, do this properly. Wonder what's properly? Wonder what time it is? It's amazing how extraordinarily infinitely interminable this is. Hummmmmmm.

Just when I thought the tube I was would calcify, the sound did change. No gong, different music, and for fifteen minutes we pushed out, we pushed in. How does one arrange this bad-energy exit, you get to wondering, in seven and a half minutes? I saw Dinah give it up and, head down, collapse as if in despair. Perhaps she was thinking of Eve's remark about getting hypnotized that I'd recounted to her on the way. Soon she will be leaving her own children. How can she? What is it about? If there is a way to know, maybe I'll find it in Poona. But if you want to scream at your mother, why don't you scream at your mother? And despair, why must it be under the auspices of this man made God? Especially if his summons is its very cause.

So few people are driven by a passion outside the ordinary paraphernalia of their lives; fewer of these still are women; almost none are women with children. Dinah's drive was always clear, and maybe someone could have prophesied its taking this form and becoming dominant, her children recessive. But having seen her spend herself so utterly on her work—with some idea of the resources required for such an effort (mainly connected with guilt for being so idle compared to this dynamo) and all the varied, vivid activities she managed without apparent strain—I can't imagine a force demanding even greater fealty from her. She's done everything, and most of it at once. In the eight years we've been friends she's not only had four successful novels published but set up a complicated commune in her new house, worked on an assembly line in a cream bun factory, organized slide shows and written pamphlets about Vietnam, traveled there, written one play and directed another, served on learned panels, stripped and refurbished a boat to sail around the canals, collaborated on a feminist film script—not to mention constantly attended meetings (women's liberation, a weekly evening with Judith and me to read our work aloud, a group to study Marx, another to read the work of Lacan—an esoteric French psychologist —a women's street-theater group, a women in Indochina group) and thrown herself into any innovative therapy that came along—and still had energy to spare to take her children on all kinds of imaginative excursions and holidays, from up the Nile to down the Alps. Just keeping track of her was exhausting, and I've never known what she was up to, entirely. She seems to think her life of such small consequence that, if you lacked the wit to address her with the right direct question—"Have you won a prize for your latest novel?" "Did you just spend a week in Devon in sensory deprivation eating only grapes?"—you'd never hear anything about it.

The only clue is in her books, so at odds with her life, so poisonous with loathing for the role the English upper classes had decreed for her. By now she has dismantled the latter down to the blood and viscera. The words come freely from her: she's spent years hacking out a direct route to her center from which to extract them—but they are alien to, or the reverse side of, her tolerant and cheerful bearing. Reading her novels was shocking, not least because they so contradicted her qualities as friend: generous, responsive, genuine, *there*. So many people need her. She needs no one.

Or so I've thought. Seeing her now, limp with sadness like a dying swan in this unlikely setting of orange, green, and undulating arms, is to realize how absolutely deficient my understanding has been.

At last! the music stops and we "may lie." It's peaceful, but sounds of children playing in the street bring on thoughts of mine, who need dinner. Finally a gong to signify the end, and people drift out. Solicitous inquiries about my "feelings," but Stuart dismisses me with a backhand tap to the middle and "That's nothing. Wait till you get to the *dynamic!*" Must I? Feeling fine, I only struggle with an overwhelming sensation of So what. Dinah's offered to take all the children camping next weekend so I can do THE REAL THING. Hummmmmmm.

June 23

After a morning of bureaucrats, bankish and other, plus a case of mini-cholera, typhoid or pox from yesterday's shots, I could use a good retreat. That, however, is not what's awaiting me. Further cautionary conversation about Bhagwan-style meditations. Liz/Anatta comes to visit, confirming the worst of Judith's and Dinah's reactions. "It's going to knock you for a *loop*," she promises enthusiastically, then suggests the many treats in store. "People get fevers and mucus, backaches and all *kinds* of pains. Any toxic that's hidden starts to flow. All you've got to do is ride with it!"

Nothing erodes my sympathy like jargon. Anatta uses so much of it so repetitively that I'm getting the hang of it. It's the kundalini in the evening and the dynamic in the morning, in which the "Hoo!" and the catharsis are the great features. Next week all sannyasins celebrate Guru-purnima Day (an annual celebration of all gurus) when the English contingent go to the seaside for "a huge kurtan" (dance meditation). There are three such holidays a year, the others being December 11 (Bhagwan's birthday) and March 21 (Bhagwan's Enlightenment Day). Anatta reels off the dates as familiarly as she can tell you the number of sandalwood beads in her mala (108, for the Hindu gods), and talks about what fun such fêtes are at the ashram, though why that should also apply in Britain is unclear since "Everything that surrounds him is a load of shit. But it's *great* to see Bhagwan. He's *great*." Will I get to see him? Well, she hears, "It's really hard to get darshan now. With so many sannyasins you have to wait a month or six weeks." How will I manage this special sort of audience then, with only three weeks? "He sees everyone arriving. Just go to Mukta." This, I am invited to understand, is someone's name. There are others who drift into her talk and leave again without making a dent on the ear, and when she gets to the "Give my love to's" I have to ask her to write them down. Vidyia and Bodi (goes the list), Deeksha and Krishna, Maneesha and Teertha, Anurada, Sagar, Ganda, Pria, Sadhu. It should be easier to attach distinct new sounds to distinct new faces but, of course, it isn't.

After she'd gone, Moby, who had known her just a year ago as Liz, asked, "Why did he change her name after her parents tried so hard to guess it?"

June 27

A visit to Judith. I love to sit in her kitchen and watch her in motion—she has such a deft relationship with *things*, and a kind of reverence for them that transcends materialism. Making a meal, she moves among the objects in a way that almost makes you forget to eat the food. The quaint labels she prizes off tins to glue to the wall, the butter dish with the cow on top, the cherrywood peppermill, the bentwood chair with the corduroy seat: they're all still here in her new bijoux lovebox—which even has separate rooms for writing and for seeing patients. But I miss the old room. It was the perfect nest where two visitors seemed a warm crowd and which was really made to fit just her. There, surrounded by her anomalous, exquisite objects, she wrote or, failing, sank into despair. She thought her downswings too terrible to inflict on anyone, and had a way of disappearing. But when the world was good to her, she danced. So light, so graceful, she was possessed by a dream goddess and all who watched her caught their breath. She danced on paper, making magic rainbow doodles, and in

talk as well: her eyes, her brilliant laugh, extraordinary at-
tenuated hands. A woman of such beauty that it seemed the
world should lie in wait and instantly embrace her—why
was she so alone? After an endless psychoanalysis, she'd
read all the orthodox work in psychology and then the
heterodox, enrolled in a university course, and finally decided to train as a psychotherapist herself. Joining
R. D. Laing's Philadelphia Association, she soon was seeing
many patients. The moods leveled out; she was obviously as
sensitive a help to all her people as she'd been in writing
and with her friends. At last she seemed to feel proud and
needed. But apart from a couple of flea-bitten, short-lived
boyfriends, still alone.

Is Bhagwan what she needs? Everything she says and
does indicates a predisposition to join the life there. How
can I even start to imagine an existence without them *both*?

It's not just the women's group where we first met eight
years ago to explore the untracked terrain of our feelings
and to become, with all the others, locked into a relationship of strange profundity and permanence. It's not the separate writing meetings, also once a week, to read aloud and
cheer each other on—although without them, my morale so
often fails. It's really all the other times, the dinners, calls,
films, shared crises, letters, walks together. How often with
Judith—there are whole streets of London that only mean
her to me. Birthdays. Though grounds for celebration were
devised with ease, we've always made a special ceremony
out of birthdays. Treated to marvelous meals, indulged and
understood, I've felt borne into my new years on waves of
tenderness. The best of these was just last year, when my
birthday coincided with the opening night in Leicester of a
play of Judith's which Dinah directed. One of the interesting features of our expedition there was the fact that we
never were exposed to the sky from the moment we left my

front door until we returned to it—Leicester having been rebuilt as a sort of giant cave city, with parking, theater, shops, hotel, and all roofed in and bathed in Musak. Within this cocoon, and unique in my life then, were two whole days of nothing but laughter and cheering and song, provoked by the kind of shorthand dialogue only possible after a bond of years. It's that above all which I can't face losing, can't think how ever to replace. Parents, children, colleagues, and conspirators, we three seem elementally intrinsic to each other's lives. And here is Judith, spooning rice into a lovely bowl, and all of it—you'd think at first—is just the same as ever. But it isn't. I am getting *mad*, insanely angry. We simply do not see or hear each other anymore. She is talking to me as the other sannyasins do, or the semi-sannyasins or would-be-sannyasins or know-it-all-about-sannyasins. "Poonam says you really ought to do some groups before you go to India."

Oh yeah? Why should I? Will pillow-punching with Poonam help Bhagwan receive me? Perceive me? Who is Poonam anyway to know what I ought to do? She doesn't even know when her own bells go off. Why should I spend whole weekends trapped among these orange people when any one of them seems as eager as Anatta to inform me of their scatological opinion of each other? Why should I have to pay strangers to listen to my complaints? What is the relevance? It's like going to an orgy because nobody loves you.

"Well, you ought to try," says Judith, tolerating me. She wants me to go to a three-day encounter group with her and Stuart next weekend while Dinah takes the children camping, and "Be prepared with a problem to solve."

"Such as?"

"Oh, say, um, what about, ah, your anger with your ex-husband?"

They really think I'm dim. They've lost contact with who-knows-what, and somehow believe in their superior insights. There's more of this than ever since Judith started her analytical training. I told her about visiting Timothy Leary at the big estate in upstate New York where he and his acid-heads resided, to hear him solemnly explaining to a CBS interviewer that if only she, too, had taken acid, she would be able to discern in the overgrowth below (we were all on the roof, he dressed togalike in a sheet) the remnants of a tennis court. The interviewer kept her face straight. What could she say? *Anyone* could see the tennis court. As far as my anger with Bernardo goes, Judith knows all about it. What's the point of hauling it out all over again before a collection of voyeurs who know nothing? It's all right now; why doesn't she know *that*? I've more or less digested it before her very eyes and ears: a hard year for my friends, but that is why they are friends. Time to move on. What about my anger with *them* for example? But then who needs pillows?

I owe them trust, though, I keep trying to remember, and they seem to think I need some basic training. I didn't tell her no, just left it there. If she pursues it, all right. Meanwhile, over her beautiful green coffee pot, "Poona is hell," Judith intones. There it is again. But

"the more you are open to all things—
if you are open to experience hell,
so you are open to heaven,"

also saith Judith, as if reciting verse.
Scream.

June 29

"The ashram *is* a rather beastly place," says Dinah. "A jungle, actually. Since Bhagwan's technique involves shaking everybody up to get rid of their repressions and release energy, there's a constant confrontation of violent emotions. The sannyasins are quite vicious to each other when they get into it."

"Why get into it? Why not stay here?"

"I'm so relieved you're coming," she says, "so I won't have to keep on trying to explain."

So here I go, a quarter the price of a roof, and not an answer to any of it, to anyone. Only Bhagwan makes sense. The more I absorb of him the more my attention builds. It would be so much easier to dismiss him; yet he is starting to surround me. Yesterday I was reading a Rajneesh newsletter while Bruno, an artist from Milan, drew pictures of me. Noticing what the newsletter was, he told me a Mulla Nasrudin anecdote (so familiar is he with the Poona scene, I am amazed to hear, that he knows of the apocryphal idiot that Bhagwan uses to leaven his talks): A wife nagged Nasrudin to get up out of bed and close the window because "it's cold outside." When finally he agreed and closed it he said, "So now it's warm outside?" (Later I am told that this is an old New York Jewish joke, but Bhagwan's sources are far-flung.) This Bruno has lost some friends to Bhagwan. You'd think Milan has been decimated, to hear him talk. He says it is impossible, no question, to go there and resist the orange. Yet when asked why he doesn't take up the challenge himself, since he seems so interested, he replies that he is not interested. He's just been to Brazil and thinks that is more interesting. Ah, but if someone gave him a ticket? "Then I would go." I promised him I would become the only person who actually came back blue.

In a pamphlet the meditation center puts out, I found the first solid information:

Bhagwan Rajneesh was born on December 11, 1931, in a small village near Jabalpur in India. He was born with full memory of his past lives and achieved enlightenment at the age of 21. For nine years he was a professor of philosophy at two Indian universities. He travelled through India giving discourses which were sometimes considered revolutionary and were certainly non-traditional. In 1966 he resigned his professorship to devote his life to the spiritual awakening of others.

He has recently moved to Poona where he lectures daily, one month in English and the next in Hindi. Many westerners go to see him and decide to become sannyasins—to adopt the spiritual path with Bhagwan as their teacher. Some stay there with him, to help in the running of the ashram and preparing books for publication. But most he sends back to the West. He says that it is necessary to be able to meditate in London or New York as easily as in a Himalayan retreat— or a Poona ashram. So there are many sannyasins now in the West, learning to meditate "in the market-place."

It is impossible to convey in words the experience of being in Bhagwan's presence. Simply, it is to experience complete acceptance and total love.

In most of the techniques devised by Bhagwan, there is a strong emphasis on using physical energy. Bhagwan stresses that there can be no separation between mind and body and that by clearing energy blocks in our body we become integrated human beings again.

Basically the theory is very simple and the concepts will be familiar to anyone who knows something of the work of Wilhelm Reich. All our neurosis is rooted somewhere in the body. At some point in our childhood we decided that in order to survive, to get the love we needed to exist, it was necessary to stop being ourselves —we had to be the way others, usually our parents, wanted us to be. At that moment we stopped being real and became phoney—and the tragedy is that we have now forgotten the reality! We couldn't allow ourselves to feel, and to stop the feelings we tensed our bodies, suppressed our needs, and stopped breathing.

In Bhagwan's meditations we are thrown back into our bodies, we start to breathe again, gradually to un-tense—and we start to feel. Of course we will resist, because it may be painful. We have spent a lifetime suppressing and to begin to experience deeply again is at first very difficult. But if we can persevere, have the courage to continue, then we gradually come to realise the vastness of our potential as human beings and the ultimate bliss which is possible for us all. To help us on this vast inner journey we need a teacher. A teacher who has made this journey himself and who is able to communicate this to others—Bhagwan is such a teacher.

Bruno says Bhagwan is not really a mystic but a first-rate intuitive psychologist, that his great talent lies in discerning the identity one most wants for oneself, and then giving it a name. "What is the most important thing about you?" he asked. I have no answer ready. "Well, Bhagwan will find out," he said. "What did he name your friend?"

"Ma Prem Pankaja. It means something like Madame Love Lotus." (Is that the most important thing about Dinah?)

I thought of what Dinah had said some time ago: "Bhagwan knows you straight away, he sees all the way through you and knows everything." This in the context of deciding that her children, after trying life in Poona for some six months and hating it—Felix wouldn't even go near the ashram—should therefore be allowed to go home, "because they are people too." "But how could he know about the children, having not even *seen* one of them?" I'd asked, and she had said, *"He can see through me to them."* Then are they really "people too" to him, or simply Dinah's children? If he really saw them he would know how much they need her. Or it seems to me they do, but perhaps I'm merely being conventionally Western in my interpretation of the look in Emily's eyes when she sees her mother. Anyway the other question is how much Dinah needs Emily and Felix, and in my observation the answer has been: Very much. Yet he never suggested that she stay with them. Just "Let them go."

"I must think of a really good question to ask Bhagwan," I mused to Bruno.

"Everyone does," he said.

The question I'd like to ask is connected to a statement in the pamphlet: "At some point in our childhood we decided that in order to survive, to get the love we needed to exist, it was necessary to stop being ourselves . . ." Of course these may be suspect as not being his own words, but presumably he acknowledges that children need love to exist; therefore why should he be the instrument of depriving Dinah's children?

July 3

My traveling companions seem in rather poor shape. I had a brainstorm yesterday and, calling Judith to talk about it, received a blast of hysteria. The inspiration came from lunch with Bill Pirie, biochemist and old friend whose work in extracting edible protein from leaves has met with little but frustration for the three decades it's been a practical possibility. He has devised a machine irreverently called a "mechanical cow," which, far more economically taking the place of that animal, might feed the world's poor; but since those poor have no money there isn't any profit in it, and all efforts to set it up fall prey to local bureaucracy and graft. Suddenly it became clear I couldn't go to India without visiting one of the few leaf-protein projects that appeared to be succeeding—Bill had told me of such a one in Coimbatore, southern India—and therefore, I suggested to Judith, I might leave earlier than they did to detour there.

She gets excitable sometimes and creates gaps—"I don't know where Dinah is" (non sequiturs aside, it's "Pankaja" when things are going well). "I haven't seen her in *days*." Resisting this line of conversation, I pursued the travel plan, and suddenly, obsessions with ashram and patients to one side, she embraced it as well: "I want to come *too!*" Fine, fine, let's *all* go.

They came over later, Dinah in a "panic" (strong word for her) which is *general* she insists and not tied in *any way* to child-leaving or the fact that she's spent two days quarreling violently with her mother but "all of it." All of what? As usual she behaves with such extravagant concern for others that in no time she manages to drift away from her own difficulties—the encounter group will deal with them, why bother me? (She never thinks people care about her except in structures.) We had dinner before Dinah left to start socking pillows at midnight—it's the same famous encounter that Judith tried to lure me to and which she'd planned to attend as well, but she's too busy planning her exit and I have nowhere to leave the kids, since Dinah's panic obviously precludes the camping plan. I'd rather go to bed anyway. They don't even let you sleep in that place. Over dinner, more ghastly revelations from Dinah.

Revelation 1. The question of signing on in advance for various groups in Poona. Stuart has already. They will be crowded. Groups? What sort of groups? Well there's So-and-So's encounter, which "even the leader himself hates," and "therefore is terrible." There's another which is quite good but it goes on for a week, from after dynamic to before kundalini every day. I cannot quite follow the drift of this, but with so little time to spend in India I hardly feel like giving up a week on this pointless (to me) activity, wasting all your perfectly reasonable revenge on an innocent foam-rubber cushion.

2. In a list of essentials—Vit. C, insect repellent, anti-malaria pills ("Paludrine not Daraprem"), chocolate, cheese—it is revealed that we must take along some special sort of face wash. Why? "It's scentless." Is that something to do with India? "No, it's Bhagwan, he can't bear scent, so there are people smelling you before you go in and if you don't pass they send you away." "But I don't smell! Do I smell?" I asked, and she gave my hair a good sniffing and failed me categorically. "Scentless shampoo, too," she instructed. That's going too far, I said, you can't seriously suggest I smell? It's only Boots Family Shampoo, and I've rinsed it *out*. "Sorry," she shrugged: "No scent." Well then, I'll just borrow whatever is needed from you that day. This man is making demands on me I do not care to indulge.

3. There is a lot of messy construction work all over the ashram as it expands. The work is done by whole families, who "camp out" there as well. "The women wear these wonderful mirrored costumes," Dinah said, "which they sell to tourists after they're worn out." The children work too. Everyone gets paid two and a half "rupes" a day. (There are sixteen rupees to the pound.) What about working now in the monsoon rains (a subject of concern to me since India experts claim it is daft to go there in the rainy season)? "They carry on." What happens to their wonderful mirrored costumes? "They've nothing else to wear anyway." What do they make of Bhagwan? "Not much, I shouldn't think." I am sickened at the idea of living amidst —and by implication supporting—such an exploitative situation, but gather that this is a diversionary concern when your target is nirvana.

Judith and I almost get Dinah to stay with us and skip the encounter. But she's paid for it already—twenty-seven pounds. Isn't that quite a lot? To "get your energy flowing"? Dinah's problems, she explains, have to do not with energy but guilt, which her ex-husband Frank and the children exacerbate when she goes to see them. But since the guilt is patently well-earned and unlikely to be dispersed by the same methods employed on childhood repressions, it would seem more sensible to confront it—why not use the time and money getting drunk with Frank instead? She has no patience for such a suggestion. "I can't. I wouldn't know what to say to him." Seems to me a better use of twenty-seven pounds to try. "No, it's not possible. It doesn't *feel* possible."

What a lot of talk there is about "feelings." What about the feelings of the women in the mirrored dresses?

July 5

Now that I'm getting into the swing of this magical mystical tour I find there's far more of it around than I'd thought. Last week I was accosted in Camden Town by a Hari Krishna person who begged me to accept the gift of a record called "India." Obviously I could not refuse. Walking off with it, however, I found myself pursued and importuned for a donation. "But you said it was a gift!" I reacted indignantly. "Suggested donation two pounds," he persisted as he ran along beside me, lonely pigtail bobbing on bald skull. I gave him two pounds. The record turns out to be an unintelligible rendition of, it says here, the voices of his sect intoning their mantra. "India"?

Another day I accepted a leaflet from the Universal Peace Mission which advertises itself as conveying "the Supreme Messages to cover every aspect of life—whether conjugal, social, political, economic or spiritual—so that everyone can be rightly guided and saved from any form of exploitation, torture, want or worry which prevents peaceful coexistence."

"Sounds a tall order," I remarked to the leaflet distributor.

"Read our books," he advised, pointing out a list in the last pages. Most of them seem to be by His Holiness Sree Sree Mentu Maharaj, among them *Holy Songs*—"Spontaneous songs come like a fountain from the heart of a great Master in his contact with different devotees. They are the stream of love, faith and light in life which energises the Spirit in anyone who listens. They are unique in the world." Other authors listed suggest that His Holiness, like Rajneesh, bestows new names on his followers. There is *Divine Dicta*, Vols I and II, by Ian MacPherson (Premananda), *Beyond All* by Mrs. Primrose Tompkins (Poroma), *My Resurrection* by Rosemary Cornford (Dayama), and *Love-Lore* ed. by Mrs. Bridget Amies (Um).

To add to the confusion, I got a call from Philadelphia from an old friend who somehow had heard I was "into gurus" and wanted me to know that she'd become a devotee of "Guru Bawa" of Sri Lanka, and that three friends of hers were due in London presently en route to their master. At least they seem to have been allowed to keep their names:

Michael, Art, and Barbara, she said. Art called up when he arrived. There wasn't time to meet, but we had a chat. He spoke with one of those middle-American voices, as awkward and brightly colored as a naïve painting. Maybe he was trying to steer me straight; at any rate I got a sales talk. "It's heavy for the mind and beautiful for the heart," he said about life on his ashram. "All the junk inside gets stirred up. He really rubs your face in your bad qualities to get rid of them. At the same time there's this incredible grace. Just being with Bawa is just a totally incredible thing. He says he's a very discarded being in the world. He's more of a father to his family than an unapproachable type of person."

"How old is he?" I asked.

Art laughed. "Oh, he's talked about things he did, like, one hundred fifty years ago."

There didn't seem much to say to this. "What do you do in the ashram?"

"It's like very unstructured. We do some farming, and sit around with Bawa, and study Tamil. That's his language."

"He doesn't speak English?"

"Not too well. He's always got an interpreter. But it doesn't matter. Just the vibration that is in his speech. Just like—compassion."

"What's so compassionate about rubbing your face in your bad qualities?"

"He's an embodiment of *all* the beautiful qualities of God. So open. So pure. You can't even describe what it is because it's nothing we have ever seen. So above and beyond anything we can apprehend. You can just look at it and praise God for it."

July 6

Dinah's getting on very badly with her children. One night a week Frank goes out and she comes to their old house to make dinner. Relations strained all around, but especially with Felix, who last night kept screaming on a variety of phony pretexts while Stuart and Dinah reasoned with him in soothing voices. "Why don't you get angry?" I asked. "I'm *not* angry," she insisted.

It's clear Felix was far more interested in effect than cause, as convincing as his horrible howls sounded—and they'd been going on all afternoon, apparently, so that Dinah and Stuart kept saying, "There there, that's enough now, you've made your point, now eat your dinner"— because whenever I spoke to him he answered quite steadily and rationally. She couldn't get him to bed before midnight, screaming and yelling. He won't forgive her. She can't handle it. She obviously wants just to leave, and since she can't yet escape physically, she's half not there.

"He wants you to react!" I shouted, barely audible above the outrage of shrieks and hoots which had retreated temporarily upstairs. I reminded her of a conversation we had last week with Judith, when all three of us had been bewailing our English upbringing and wishing we were Mediterranean and had learned to fight with love instead of evading all emotional expression if there were any danger of its becoming "unpleasant." "Why can't you fight with him instead of saving it all for some group? What's it for, then?" She has an ambiguous shrug for such moments, suggesting either that *I* wouldn't understand or that she is so hopelessly inadequate that how could I expect *her* to understand. It fixes the conversation, whatever it means.

I just wish I could put her back together again, even in my own head. The Poona experience seems to have disequipped her for other life, for "real" life. The only possible comfort is speculative—maybe in the Bhagwanian version of the omelet-making recipe, it is necessary to be in such a dismembered state en route to reconstruction. But when I remember the busy, engaged, courageous, and cheerful Dinah of only a year ago (although she promises it was all a fake, it *worked*) I feel sad and muddled. She is taut with anxiety and failure-feelings and insists she needs to go to groups to cry and yell. But when will it be possible for her to cry and yell in context?

July 7

The first of the dynamic meditations. I fear not the last. Beginners' group. Arrived too late to hear the explanatory talk, so Poonam assigned a volunteer sannyasin to fill me in: "Ten minutes Chaotic Breathing, ten minutes of Catharsis, then Bhagwan's voice says 'Stop!' and you freeze for ten minutes, you know, like statues, then ten minutes of dancing." What all this meant in action, I guessed you learned in action. I got quite left out anyway. They shut the windows because of the neighbors, who might be offended by the screaming. (In Poona, Anatta reports, the police came because of the noise and now you have to "mime-scream.")

A racing, frantic samba beats out, and instantly the people chuff to it like trains, malas slung like bandoliers around one shoulder. With all of us hyperventilating, there was soon nothing left to breathe except the suffocating stink of thirty or forty bodies either robed in borrowed sweaty gowns or underpanted and heaving their unbathed flesh around. Scentlessness is only prized in Poona, I guess. Breathing only through my nose made me sick, and only through my mouth had an odd effect on the equilibrium. To get another focus I looked out from under my blindfold but the demoniac sounds gained no meaning with the view. It was my literal purgatory: They have found it! I discovered a matching bedlam described in *The Hobbit*, reading to the children later: "The yells and yammering, croaking, jibbering and jabbering; howls, growls and curses; shrieking and skriking, that followed were beyond description. Several hundred wild cats and wolves being roasted slowly alive together would not have compared with it."

For me this followed an exhausting day of work, kids, guests, shopping, cooking, and driving all over London so that even the pressure on the accelerator to get there took my last resources, and I simply had nothing left to cathart. For a while I tried to summon my own demons, but how could any match the ones before me? So I threw my smelly blindfold down and watched, stunned, trying to weave about in a token way. Ah, it's the hoo I left out, which is the yelling of Hoo! Hoo! with each exhalation following the catharsis, from which it is otherwise indistinguishable. The music might be different but it's inaudible anyway—the din quite deafening, the air like solid soup, so that I could only wonder which would give out first, my top or my middle: Would it make me mad or sick? And what about that face, in constant punctuating view? This way Bhagwan smiles benignly down; over there the poster has him younger with his hair still black. Another picture shows him gazing with Significance and Mystery; a fourth directly laughs and challenges: spin, whirl, turn, you cannot get away.

Stop such thoughts. Concentrate on the activity: amazing. One girl's robe had split to her pelvis, which she exhibited writhing to any (many) being disobedient with their blindfolds; a man leapt about clad in nothing *but* his blindfold, his penis doing a dance of its own; another girl had one breast out. All exposed parts were comely, as if even this degree of abandonment still takes account of esthetics and/or narcissism, so the pubis on show is blond, the breast centerfold material, the cock an inordinate length, but their owners at least remained sightless. The concern seems to be of self as performer in a ritual display (even if to an ostensibly blind audience)—but never the slightest hint of relationship, of anyone to any other. Exposing and revealing oneself en masse but alone and on cue, an extension of the dance of our times.

There is something disoriented or misoriented here that bothers me. The state of being *sent* is one thing, recognizable and human, but the ability to turn it on and off at ten-minute intervals, according to an order or a shift in the music, is another. I have seen normally staid Englishmen driven to insensibility in a fundamentalist trance, Syrian dervishes whirling on fire, Brazilian Candomble dancers re-

ceiving their gods and becoming them, American Holy
Rollers possessed of alien voices and spirits, Mexicans
dragging themselves on shredded, bleeding knees along
miles of rocky paths toward their saint, the ululations of
Arab women ferocious with torment or joy—and in all of
these have found some beauty, in their relationship to each
other and their source. Even when the dancer or the trancer
is quite alone, he is possessed with something other than
Self. These people seem obsessed with self: each one extracting from his insides the pain and rottenness as a sort of
offering for its own sake. But what kind of pain comes on
with a gong?

They offer mint tea and the chance to ask Poonam some
questions. A man wants to know "how can men go about
being orange if they have respectable jobs? Women," he
points out, "can look perfectly normal, just the same thing
only orange. But how can I get an orange three-piece suit?"
It is suggested that he have one made. He is annoyed, that
isn't what he meant—but then so few sannyasins have a
respectable-job problem. It points up the unfairness to me
for women too—you can look normal, even glamorous, but
it's expensive and indulgent and very unholy to me, throw-
ing out your entire wardrobe (Dinah passed her nicest
things on to me) and spending weeks pursuing rumored
orange jeans or belts or socks.
There follows a taped lecture on—ironically enough
considering my earlier speculations—Relationships. Bhagwan's voice surprises me with its high pitch and mispronun-
ciation of the fancy words. There is also a problem with
the sibilants. "Possess" sounds like "purchase." "Rubbis-s-s,"
he says, and "bullsit." I suppose I expected a holy rumble,
the echo-chambered voice of God in a Cecil B. De Mille
movie. Hard to follow after reading him, which I prefer,

and soon I doze off. Waking as the tape ends, feeling lovely for the first time all day, I am congratulated by Dinah for falling asleep. I'd hoped they might not notice. But it turns out "Bhagwan loves it when you sleep as he is talking. It's the best way to absorb his energy."

At dinner at the local Greeks', Dinah tells me about her energy theory. Bad, good, the way in, the way out: *every-thing is energy*. I recall someone a decade ago—interesting under these circumstances—as earnestly explaining that *every*thing is guilt. My response to Dinah is a kind of So? Yes? Go on?—but that, it turns out, is that. And all at once I realize it's happening again: Dinah, inspired by her misery, is answering yet another question I have not asked. Or whose answer hardly seems worth remarking. This is becoming so routine these days I hardly dare hope for some validity in the only alternative explanation—that I don't need to ask.

For instance, Dinah often talks of the need to avoid repression but to "watch" your anger and "drop it." In my view, if your negative emotions have a cause, it's of interest to scrutinize the cause, not the emotions. For one thing, if you do not dwell on pain, far from inspiring questions, the pain seems to diminish. If you *can't* dwell on it because you have too much to do in dealing with its source, you tend to become less preoccupied with your suffering and more with your doing (and often a remedy suggests itself, glancing off another surface). But among the sannyasins, their suffering and their doing are the same thing. Their pain is their premise, occupation, raison d'être: they are going through it, straightest possible route, as Bhagwan says to do. You cannot comfort them, they won't allow it. And how can you suggest alternatives, in a very loud voice at any rate, to people whose entire lives are dedicated to this search? It's as if they're busy trying out a vast collection of skeleton keys on some door they've encountered, exchanging strategems and names of locksmiths, when if they'd look they'd see it hadn't any hinges and would give with the merest push. No, that can't be—there is such pity for me in their eyes, they must know something I don't.

". . . Wasn't *that* something?" Dinah was asking about the dynamic, licking taramosalata off her mala. Lots of curiosity, breathless leaning forward seeking affirmation, how'd I feel, how'd it go, did I en*joy* it? and I mumbled that I'd actually spent the best part lying down (having cunningly contrived to be prone at the moment of Freeze) and that I seem incapable of producing my bedlam, whatever it may be, in this way—I hadn't probably given it what was required, since I hadn't *felt* like it. Hoped that would do. Sounded Bhagwanian enough, anyway. But here is the contradiction: He says to do what you feel, but you are told to do what I don't feel.

Later

It's not that my life is painless. (Though arguably my pain is increasingly lifeless.) It's not hard to isolate the sources of this pain, or to examine them, or even to consider what solutions I have found or still hope to find; but there is no relief or connection somehow at the

Rajneesh Centre. What is offered indisputably helps Judith and Dinah, and so immerses them that it is as if we live in separate elements now. The different things we think about no longer touch. Where once we merged, we're hardly capable of tangents anymore. Maybe above all this hurts most.

Pain to me is a kind of loneliness. There are many kinds. Years of marriage muddled up in memory produce this probable exaggeration: When I was married I was never alone and always lonely. Now I am often alone and seldom lonely. I like being alone, so long as I have work to do and people to call on after dark. But being *lonely-together* can go quite past pain to torture. The necessary pretense is such a mockery and, double-edged, it cuts you both ways. Half the time you're laughing bitterly at yourself: Ha *Ha!* the echoes boom around the hollow room—because although the room contains another person, and the children and the cat, no one understands the joke. The joke *is* the joke, and that is loneliness—hearing your own laughter at yourself for laughing at yourself. Assorted eaveslookers, warmed by the sight of the family in their nest and otherwise conscientiously oblivious, concluded that the scene was cozy, enviable. They neither helped nor interfered; they did not think it their place. In fact you couldn't expect them to. Certainly not to meddle with a Wife. You're not supposed to turn to others after you're a Wife; protocol requires you direct your life through his. "If you are a married woman living with your husband," writes H. M. Inland Revenue, "he should complete the form as if it were addressed to him." My friends, of course, were above all that. Ha *Ha!*

They sat around the kitchen table, helping nothing but the years go by, enthusiastically promoting the pretense so much they didn't even care it was one—which made me have to work at it even harder. Lots of people moved into our marriage, sat around like sponges absorbing their own idea of what was going on. They felt wonderful. They beamed. They had tremendous appetites. They drank a lot and stayed half the night. Some of them even moved in. Now and then they were diverting enough to encourage; usually their illusions covered me like weights that keep a diver on the bottom of the sea. Not drowning, but waving, certainly, and no one *saw*—except my women's group, and especially Dinah and Judith. Judith because she was so sensitive when she cared; Dinah because she was a wife too, even if a very different kind, and there seemed to be no pain that eluded her. It's a species of problem without much relation to the personalities involved, though certainly aggravated by having the right children (one of each sex); the right sort of pets, smells in the kitchen, toys on the stairs, muddy boots in the hall, eccentric old car—that whole caboodle suggesting friendly chaos, homely joy, and generosity of spirit, all the bits of trap which you yourself have painstakingly and deliberately set, and which have to hold together (fingers crossed) or you will die. You'll die because you're no more self-sustaining than a single muddy boot: you're merely part of this ghastly charade, and all of it depends on all the rest of it.

When we were playing house with our baby in New York, our last phone number, if you changed the digits into letters (the fashion then), spelled CHARADO.

How can such a poised hairspring of a life continue, especially if you actually don't want it to? But when it does give way, the expected panic still ensues. The trap is sprung right on your tenderest parts—your insane delusions. Without them, what? Betrayal, uselessness, envy, jealousy, hatred, self-hatred, pathos, bathos, Minsk, Pinsk—the caboodle is up and with it, you. Nobody loves me, everybody's pointing at me, why should I even get up, I'm dying.

It has to be that way, because for years, it was fear of *this* happening that kept *that* happening. Therefore this has to be terrible, or otherwise why were you fooling yourself for so long about how terrible it would be?

But what if it isn't? a small bubble surfaces one day. *What if I am fine?* Come to think of it, I do believe I'm fine. I'm not a boot. I never was. I have worn my sorrow like a habit. A bad habit. Why not give it up?

What a revolutionary notion.

Dinah and Judith do not see it that way. Everything they say and do with their faces conveys undercurrents of dis-approval, as if I've joined the maniacal pull-yourself-together cold-shower crowd; as if I am evading something by not being miserable. It couldn't be that simple, I must be covering up. In deference to my recently delicate state, they do not speak directly of these things (this is the worst of it): they seem instead to be intent on midwifing me toward and through the inevitable day when I will come to my senses and feel good and rotten again, so we can all feel good and rotten together and delve and grovel in it. Meanwhile they treat me with this tolerant forbearance as if I'm being *brave*, which would not be so insulting if I didn't know that in their frame of mind, such a verdict is equivalent to *dishonest*.

Now I am lonely-together with Dinah and Judith.

July 14

It is Judith's birthday. I have got her lots of wacky little gifts, and tonight we celebrate at Manzi's. I must ask Dinah what we do about her birthday now. Theoretically she has a new one, the date of taking sannyas.

I was talking to some visiting Americans about Laing, and learned something behind my words. So many friends and neighbors either work with him in the Philadelphia Association or admire him to distraction, that I have often gone to hear him speak, and been overwhelmed with his formidable concentration, the mesmerizing effect of his talk regardless of its content: as if he were permitting us brief access to his strange stream of thought, bothering to speak it aloud for a while (usually to raise money for the P.A.) but essentially conveying his uninterrupted process—and his process (not without some humility on his part) has become his mistaken idea of his power. His followers are too often unable to develop and use his ideas because the ideas seem less fruitful in themselves than when Laing himself applies them. An idea is perhaps as valid as the extent to which its followers, as opposed to its initiator, can use it (as Christ's, Marx's and Freud's ideas survived their own application of them—though it would be hard in many cases to recognize the relationship in the mutant results). In

Laing's case there are perhaps a hundred steady sycophants who refer to themselves rather sinisterly as "the network," regularly block the front rows of his lectures, give him a distorted view of his communicative force because they are such yes-men, and isolate him from his peers. But has he any peers? I saw him share a platform with one, Gregory Bateson, and Laing's claque rudely buzzed and twitched and showed more interest in a heckler than in Bateson. Their incapacity to listen showed how little contact they had with the content of this level of thinking, unless expounded by their leader personally.

Part of my resentment of them, I recognize, is envy. I am as vulnerable as anyone to this kind of power. Fidel did it to me in Cuba. Five minutes after he began his May Day speech, I had forgotten my name. I have often wondered how resistant I'd have been to Hitler. Laing can talk about absolutely anything and give you the idea that he is some sort of conduit to the infinite. You feel part of a conspiracy of mutual hallucination. Yet I have exchanged glances with him frequently over a transfer of children (as members of the same school carpool) and he has never *looked* at me. What if he had? What if Fidel had? What now when I am to be subjected to the—obviously very similar—powers of this Bhagwan, with not only the same kind of *presence* but also the ability—according even to the skeptical—to "see you as you really are." He has, at latest count, sixty thousand sannyasins who are eagerly, ineptly spreading the word. Like Laing, Bhagwan must be measured ultimately by the effectiveness of his ideas as applied by others. Meanwhile here is the chance to see him apply them himself.

But how on earth, if I was so seduced by Laing, can I possibly resist Bhagwan? Madness. Perhaps Bruno is right, why take the test?

But as Bruno admits, even he'd go with a free ticket.

July 22

The sun is shining through the leaves of the magic rowan tree, the tomatoes are growing, I have just made love after a delicious lunch, no one is here and it is quiet. To appreciate this is enough.

But to sit at my desk means moving the calendar forward eight days (turning the dial eight times though once would have done) and feeling guilty because I haven't written anything for that long.

This proves that something is wrong with me. Not only failing to achieve anything, but feeling guilty about it.

But is that bad?

Can Bhagwan make you feel less guilty because you have been enjoying-yourself instead of enjoying-yourself-productively? Productive meaning qualitatively creative—though there is the question of who is assessing the result. For example, I think very highly of my laundry arrangement. Gazing at the clothes I've hung to dry, I see how beautiful they are: the way the colors pick each other out, the shapes of shirts in line, a row of socks in pairs, a yellow sweater waving from the back. If a man had painted that on canvas, they'd put it on a wall and everyone would toast it with red wine. But laundry! Laundry is a drudge, despised by men.

No credit. Is it any less creative, lacking credit? Is anybody out there interested? Bhagwan?

At first there was a lot of talk about dying clothes. Recipes were exchanged of the different mixtures of Dylon needed to achieve oranges so subtle you might actually take them for ochre or purplish brown. Jockeying between washing machines, we resolved on Dinah's because she had to be with her kids on the chosen day; then I couldn't come so she said never mind, there was lots more to do anyway and we'd set another day. Yesterday I collected a book Dinah had left for me with Judith and noticed next to it a tin of dye. When I asked Judith if there were more oranging coming up she said No, they'd finished. Well, I mean to say, what's it to me? I don't want to be anybody's sannyasin. It was bad enough to be a wife (and that, indeed, of a man named orange in various Slavic languages). But Judith hurt me, saying that. Hurt from being excluded from what you've chosen to exclude yourself? No madder than the outlandish fantasy I cultivated next, that perhaps they do not want me to join them in their sannyas, that the very point of me for them may be to reject it well (reject it but reject it *well*), as a way of helping them to be free too. Oh, rubbish. Besides there is a much better explanation than such altruism: its opposite. Although everybody doing what they want, à la Bhagwan, contains, as usual in my case, the possibility of going wrong since so often what I want is simply what I do. With the definite exception of the dynamic meditation.

July 24

Last-minute frenzied operations to cope with packing in no suitcases with the children home on holiday and entertaining everyone they know with game of Rearrange the Debris. I am so depressed about getting this show on the road that it's almost a relief my traveling companion is a professional shrink. (Joke.) However, last night the final before-the-summer women's group dinner led to a violent row in which I found myself on the (tactically) wrong side, so that everything seems thrown in doubt.

The subject was death. Dinah told of a woman who died of a brain tumor at the ashram this spring. She had been renamed "Vipassana" by Bhagwan—Sanskrit for "consciousness of breath," and meant to show great prescience on his part. The event took place over a matter of days. Bhagwan urged his sannyasins to sit with her at her deathbed and to meditate about its significance; afterward they had an Indian ceremonial pyre on a ghat and everybody danced while the body burned. Dinah found the experience a revelation. She no longer feared death, she said, but had learned to see it as part of an inevitable cycle of birth and rebirth. Our painful Western attitudes had always caused her terror, and now she feels a great release from these anxieties, indeed a profound acceptance.

Carolyn led the chorus of outrage which followed. This is all very fine, she maintained, to people with our luxury of choice, but to those who have never been without hunger and drastically premature death it has the ring of a ruling-class rationale. Consider the relationship to our own struggle—women who joined together to affirm their own identities in the context of centuries of male mystification: Just as it is helpful to men if we believe ourselves elevated when we are in fact held down, it is useful to convince the Indians that death holds no terrors since they'll probably watch most of their children die, and push off themselves, before they even reach the average age of us women around the table. Especially with the built-in frill of the expectation of elevation in the next life.

Nothing could sway Dinah and—by a now inevitable extension—Judith. It is imperialist, Dinah stated, to inter-pret other people's lives in terms of your own. If you do not fear death, starvation has a different meaning. Groans, anger, childish shouting. "Ask a maimed beggar how he feels!" "Ask yourself!" I tried to rephrase Carolyn's propo-sition in less tendentious language. When they still resisted even to address it, I heard myself hissing at them: "*I can't see how we can travel together!*" and Dinah, ordinarily the mildest of women, snarling back "Nor can I!" From Judith, whose parents were once communists and who grew up within this sort of vocabulary, the refusal to see—she ar-gued in language as strident as Carolyn's: the neophyte's dogmatism—is even more baffling. But the talk fragmented as all expressed themselves at once; only later, after the furies had died down (coinciding with the exit of the angri-est), did it become apparent that Dinah had struck a vein of deep anxiety in us all. Perhaps it's true that she "no longer fears death," but, considering her unusual loss of control, this seems unlikely; certainly the rest of us found it hard to discuss with any serenity. We've always made brave noises about aging, but how ready are we really for old age, let alone death? The idea arose to start a Death Club (provoking various faces to wince and cringe)—to stay together and to help each other die, with informed support from a thorough understanding of our needs and wants. We drew calm immediately from the idea—except Judith, who thought it was disgusting.

Meanwhile, Poona news. Stuart (a.k.a. "Swami Devopama") has arrived there and plunged instantly into a "primal therapy group"—two weeks to shake his world. He can write notes, but when we get there next week he won't be allowed to talk to us. "Terribly inconvenient of him," snips Dinah. "He might have waited." However, it does help justify the lovely sidetrip I've concocted for us, to include Madras on the way to the mechanical cow in Coimbatore; which in turn provides Stuart with the "space" he says he needs. Poor thing was denied entry to his first darshan due to smelly hair (baby shampoo). (When I told Ed Doctorow the other day about Bhagwan's idiosyncratic smell and touch problem, he remarked: "Sounds like Howard Hughes." Also J. Edgar Hoover. A rum company.)

July 27

There was some mistake about the tickets. Dinah has left for Poona and will return to Bombay to meet us. I wish she hadn't. As peculiar as she is these days, she still represents a ballast of sorts.

Having dispatched my children with labels round their necks to Portugal, feeling bereft and savoring it, I return from the airport to Anatta on the doorstep and an endless ringing of the bell, all faces stamped URGENT and delivering speeches, requests, advice, addresses, premonitions, admonitions, *threats*. If I were off to Sicily or Singapore would they behave this way? Each has a sentence of weight and finality to pronounce, their own particular caveat, which, before I desert them for some new life (their version), *is to be taken into account*.

Bill Mason, a Scottish artist/therapist who can handle anything, sounds distinctly threatened by this guru business. Thumbing through some Rajneesh literature on the table, he reads with a mocking lilt, "I am the beginning of a tradition, not the end. I have worked with many Masters, but I have never been a disciple." Bill snorts, "How can you be a leader if ye've never been a follower? Can ye tell me that? And they do those groups out there, do they?" His work has led him to the belief that "encounters make people *crazy*. It raises the demons and there they all are, floating about," he says, gesticulating demons in the air. "Same as psychiatrists. They're very good at raising demons and giving them a name, but no bloody use at dealing with them." All he wants to know is if I really think I'm strong enough to resist. "I'm not strong at all, but I'm pretty resilient. That's better, isn't it? Strong things break." "*Don't lose the thread!*" he bellows—Bill believes there is a thread through to the past, to other lives, but "how can you keep the thread if you change your name?"

Then I get a tongue lashing from John, who knows something of Indian mysticism, and who wants me to understand that most of these gurus so beloved by Westerners are nothing but corrupters of their tradition. An ashram is supposed to be a place of solitude, an isolated hermitage where a genuine sannyasin may eventually reside to meditate—but only after enduring a pilgrimage of a full year when, equipped with nothing but a loincloth and a begging bowl, he seeks another sort of enlightenment than that dished out by flashy frauds like this Bhagwan. " 'Bhagwan' means 'God,' you know," he says. "What sort of guru calls himself God?" ("Shree," he answers my next question, means "Mister." God Mister?)

The next bell is the phone: the modulated tones of my pal Helen, a scrounger with an Oxford education. "Seems a rather—*dic*ey business," she warns, trying hard for tact. She knows "a lot of people who had *aw*fully good sense" who, after a dose of ashram, "came back vacant and disoriented." What people? "Oh, sort of *odd* people I've met in houses in Hampstead. When you speak to them they don't seem to hear what you say." As for me, "Well, perhaps you're grounded enough not to—*real*ly take off. But they'll blow you full of hot air."

Which will be no doubt seductive, says Persian singer Shusha. "Those people are so self-obsessed that they need a license to think about themselves twenty-four hours a day. Is that you?"

My mother is next. She is aglow about my trip. Her first reaction was true to type, considering her English class background: "Of course you've heard of Poona. Poona is the hill station where the ladies of the raj went for the monsoon to have affairs with the young officers who were sent to guard them." Her second reaction (when I'd told her about Dinah) was, "I must say, anyone who's given up their children has given up the world." The third (after I mentioned that, should I make any similarly rash decision, it was *de rigueur* for her to fly out to rescue me for the sake of the grandchildren) was, "Oh, but they could live with me!" Ever since, she's simply been engaged in clearing up the details, entirely ignoring my repeated "I was only kidding"s. Today she is musing on the lines of "Eve is so easy to manage, but wouldn't Moby need a man about?" etc. Do I need this?

Then there's Dave, our local pharmaceutical expert. "You'll get the shits out there. Take this." He thrusts a bottle at me labeled Lomotil, prescribed by R. D. Laing no less. As for perils to my psyche and my children, he's easy; in fact his is the only reaction that doesn't crawl all over me: "What an exciting chance, to be able to see such a place!"

Punchdrunk, I sit out the final scene with Gilda—a Brazilian who has just completed the Fischer-Hoffman "process" in self-realization—plucking invisible boils from her arms in a demonstration of alpha and beta consciousness to, of all people, Carolyn. Carolyn is rather more concerned that my head is on the block of the ruling classes; but at least she seems to think I'll come back intact. Another left-wing stalwart has announced that not only will I inevitably "succumb" but that she will not traffic with me further "if" I do (like my sister who writes sarcastically from Paris, "Can imagine you with long Indian scarves floating around your bald head. Let me know once you feel something. If you stay in Poona for good, don't forget to say where that is."). "Oh God!" howls Michelene the poet. "Be careful! All sorts of sensible people get there and go orange and NEVER COME BACK!"

What can be the matter with everyone? If they didn't keep on as though it were some kind of spiritual virginity that was threatened, would I worry so much about "succumbing"? What I do worry about nobody mentions, except I. F. Stone at a party the other night. He alone is interested in the Pirie-protein work. As for giving up one's children, he said, "It sounds like complete insanity to me," and then brought out the one point that *promises* me pain:

"When you see India and the suffering of its people, it is very hard to understand the extraordinarily numb indifference represented as much by the spiritualists as by the Indian upper classes." Most of the Poona-bound avoid this conflict by simply sidestepping it, experiencing no more of India than you need to get from the airport to the Holy See/Hear/Speak-no-evil Bhagwan Shree. But why should it be sidestepped here, by these intelligent people? I suppose they just take it for granted. I am rather shaken that they don't take my stability or sense for granted.

Whatever has tilted the once-level heads of my friends, the condition is a major seismographic disturbance in the person of Polly. Judith has arranged for her to drive us to the airport in return for use of car. Once a member of our women's group, Polly found it insufficiently radical and moved to more forthright revolutionary activity, joining a commune which in the service of its political discipline demanded such rigorous disregard of vanity as to ban mirrors and lavatory doors; and also such contempt for personal property (even children) that all clothes had to be heaped on the floor and put on, whatever their size, as they surfaced—requiring the sacrifice of Polly's worn and very wonderful jeans. Next she got active in gay politics, rejecting males in all roles but procreative. Now this person is sitting here and telling me that she is "seriously leaning toward Bhagwan." (If that's where people like Polly arrive, why did they bother to lock up the Angry Brigade? To jail and kill the Baader-Meinhof people? Left alone they'd be in Poona by now.) She is encouraged by a friend of hers who's gone to the ashram and reported—Polly quotes in a voice like a sunrise—"It's like shedding tinted spectacles! We've constantly been making the mistake of looking at the world only through the glasses of the women's movement or radical or gay politics or whatever, but Bhagwan represents the only *real* way toward change!" Polly's one reservation is that Bhagwan is a male—her friends might never forgive her for following a man. Otherwise, she laments that she cannot join us now but must finish her acupuncture course.

I am stunned. Here we are at dawn in a nearly empty Heathrow lounge, Judith and I swallowing record amounts of coffee on the unverified theory that there isn't any in India (Polly declines, it's not macrobiotic), and already the elements of this voyage are too much for me. By the time we're on the plane it feels rhythmically more an end—or at least some climactic point—than merely the beginning. And reconciling contradictions with Judith as interlocutor is no help either. Any doubt about where we're headed or the relative goddiness of its centerpiece gets from her (already orange) the exact phrase Anatta sent me off with yesterday, spoken with the same jolly patronage: "I know just how you feel. I used to feel that way too." I would like to shriek and push her out of the plane. Instead we merely gaze rapturously at the view down and out, of blobs of smoke, woolly clouds shining in relief against their own shadows on the water beneath. Judith, staring, says "Honestly! If you look at it for a while you can start to meditate and it gets quite trippy." It's hard to bear, this new turn in her. Such a short time ago it seems since we pilgrims, Judith and Dinah and I, did meet each week to read aloud to one another our efforts in the English language. We've had years and tears and acid trips together. Am I allowed to miss the old days? "Definitely not," snaps Judith. "Be Here Now."

Aren't we getting a little dogmatic about this? The great feature of Being Here Now is what simple good advice it is. I remember another plane once, taking me away to a year in the Middle East. I was so scared that in order to go through with it at all I realized I would have to break it down and never think beyond: Today I buy a ticket. Today I pack. Now get a taxi. Tell him the airport. Get on the plane. As a tactic, it defeated fear. It's also useful in revolting situations, such as last week when I overturned the coffee pot and the kitchen floor was deluged with black muck. In the end I had a lovely time with the mop, making patterns out of mounds of grounds. The world can be a series of little wonders. I always thought of it as Dividing Everything Into Its Smallest Units. Maybe not poetry, but isn't it the same thing? A device by any name, and it can't be made to cover every situation. Present actions have future consequences. Failure to consider this leads to every kind of mess. I could make a Be-Here-Now Atrocity Collection, in fact. It would start with a few pregnancies that come to mind, and extend to such trivia as the way I ruined all my clothes when mini-skirts were fashionable.

Being Here Now, indeed, can be simply an evasion—if the only one that makes many moments endurable. I heard that Sir Julian Huxley, after having shock treatment in his advanced years, said, "It was really good to have my memory erased. I am so old I had too much of it anyway. I wasn't *bored* any more." Outside the sanctuary of the constant present tense one is forced to find the value in a moment, and if it's absent, get out. You have to judge, direct, consider implications, learn from the past or be crippled by it, invent the future, be responsible for people and events which don't necessarily confront you. Take Bill Pirie. Not only is he involved very much in the Where-When—since most of his work awaits empirical justification—but he's *happy* in it. There he is, messing around with other people's lives in order to lengthen them, when it's just their rotten karma if they're starving.

July 28

Emerging into the Bombay dawn is like merging with it: stepping into a warm bath, except that a bath is warm compared to something else, and here there's nothing else. The so-called air blends straight into instant sweat; the whole world is wet and body temperature. Yet 6 A.M. must surely be the cooler part of day? I'm not constructed for this. No wonder I avoided this place all these years. The airport interior, not an improvement, smells like the London Rajneesh Centre after a dynamic meditation. A customs officer confronts us wearing epaulets on her whitish sari. "Where are you going? Poona? Are you going to see that Rajneesh?" She titters at us, chalking bags okay.

Forging through the din and brawl, Judith and I try to get our bearings. Dinah said to sleep it off at the Airport Plaza Hotel where she'd meet us later, but we're obviously too tired to get there, and anyway the way out appears quite blocked. Beyond a wall of solid window at the far end of the hall the ground level sinks, and all you can see are hundreds of hands clawing at the glass. Closer, their predatory threat dissolves: they are attached to people meeting travelers and porters competing with each other. Yet the impression persists of supplicants, mendicants, cheats. We change some money, trying to keep attached to our bags. The men who grab at them may only be porters, but if I was as poor as they are I'd be after my suitcase (full, not of orange clothes, but of oranges, which Anatta advised were unobtainable and prized).

An exit door exists and even an "Airport Plaza" bus. The hotel is only minutes away down a mud track through soft wet jungle, outsize foliage with huge birds flapping about and a billboard signed I. Gandhi proclaiming THE ONLY MAGIC: HARD WORK FARSIGHTEDNESS DETERMINATION. The hotel is not so much air-conditioned as insect-repellent-conditioned, the exudations of the vents so thick with chemicals they gum up your throat; and the shower, basin, and other orifices contain golfball-sized mothballs (to ward off *what?*). Never mind, the only magic: sleep.

We are wakened by Dinah who sweeps in wearing a Tibetan orange robe and, apologetic and nannyish at once, announces that we can get train tickets to Madras if we make it to the station by two; a splendid chap at the tourist office there has promised to save us first-class reservations. Dinah laughs and laughs at my suitcase full of oranges and heads straight for the shower, which soon emits gurgles and swooning noises. She preceded us to India by just three days. What are the washing arrangements at her bungalow if a shower is such an event? "They turn the water off in Poon," she's saying waterily, "during the day."

"*All* day?"

"Mm."

"*Every* day?"

"Mm."

"Why?"

"Not sure. Save water I spose."

"But it's the monsoon. It rains all the time."

61

"That's true. The shower there is broken down anyway."
Oh yes? "Water heater too." Someone's meant to be mending everything, she assures us. "It's just that they don't get round to it."

We take a taxi outside: "V.T." Dinah orders, "veddy quickly please." Her voice assumes a grande-dame commandeering tone I've never heard. It makes me quite glad to be her friend. But there isn't time to think about that for long.

The first view of urban India is surely the worst sight in the world. It can never again be so shocking; one could not survive the repetition of its first assault on the senses. The degradation and the hopeless hordes are so beyond the worst expectations that there is no armor, no protection possible. The first time. But Dinah appears immune next to Judith who is crying, and in a day or two will we not notice either?

Beside me the driver is barefoot. Perhaps it gives him extra sensitivity on the pedals for his hair's-breadth escapes from certain doom, which occur about once a block. It is a wonder he can see, having festooned the car, sun visor to dashboard, with garlands of limp, yesterday's flowers. But blindly or not, he surges through the competition—a choke of pedestrians and cows, bikes and motorbikes, horse- and man-drawn carts, buses and many brightly painted trucks announcing on their rears HORN OK PLEASE—advice adhered to universally. Indeed a child might take the noise for the propellant—we never stop tooting as we overtake whatever's in the way, blast of outrage in return, multiple missings-by-an-inch. It is amazing to be so near disaster and to so barely feel it, because everyone in view is so much nearer a disaster that is more potent still. How can they be alive? So many people! When we stop at a red light (the driver turning off the motor to conserve petrol) they swoop on us crying "Ma! Ma! Ma!": the skeletal, the blind, tiny children carrying still tinier ones, many with the reddish hair of kwashiorkor, mutilated stumps poking through the window, a vast humiliation grown stoic with need—for when you put a coin in a hand, the hand does not retreat to make room for another, but instantly returns. You have to keep the windows shut against them finally, or they will not let you drive away; then open them quickly for the brief forward sprints or the heat is unendurable.

Like Egypt but more and worse. I never expected to see anything as squalid as Cairo and the amputated limbs of children (the better to beg); as Upper Egypt and the people living in and out of mud, and the trachoma killing the eyes of the villagers there; as the open sewers in a Canton back street in 1957; as the hopeless pueblos of Mexico where nothing is more than a single remove from dust. But this is in another league. If not qualitatively worse off, then quantitatively: with these numbers of people there is so clearly nothing to do. It has gone too far. Billboards bearing slogans suggesting activity and hope make a travesty of a tragedy. INDIA SUCCEEDS AGAINST INFLATION. THE COUNTRY IS ON THE MOVE.

Eccentric details arrest and distract me from the human horror everywhere. A shabby, once grand building is signposted ENGLISH MEDIUM on one side, MARATHI MEDIUM on the other. What can they mean? Voluptuous cinema advertisements display a couple at it on a bed of apples, and other entangled pairs as unlikely to appear on the censored Indian screen but apparently allowed on posters. The faces of the film stars are plump and pink of cheek, a different race of people from the emaciated dark-brown urchin running along next to us heaving with what looks to be his last strength a bus-length cart laden with hardware and bamboo scaffolding. An actual bus, double-decker like the ones in

London, is so fully packed that it seems a many-limbed Bosch creature from hell, and the rear platform only just clears the street. Some have their carts pulled by bullocks, with horns lacquered crimson and wearing bells and patch-work coverlets. But most walk, spindly men and women and children bearing burdens three or four times their own bulk on their heads. Everyone blocks the road: pedestrians dawdle about wherever they want, traffic or not; thus more hooting. Ornate remembrances of the raj or a crumbling Mughal temple, or now and then a silken-saried lady with a paunchy escort, stand out against the dereliction and exhaustion of it all.

Downtown the buildings have a gingerbread luxuriance, surrounded with palm trees and flowering shrubs. We make it to what Forster called "that oddest portal," the gargoyled and Gothic Victoria Terminus, with twenty minutes to spare before the threatened sale of our reservations. But at the tourist office no one knows where Dinah's splendid Mr. D'Souza has gone, and when he eventually appears he vaguely proposes three lovely second-class seats and evidently there is no point in asking what became of our first-class ones. In any event "You must learn the Indian way to travel" he singsongs cheerfully. It's certainly cheaper, especially with student concessions. But to find the bureau where they issue these is another story. Trekking through interminable corridors—warrens of desks and shelves nearly toppling under the weight of stacks of frayed brown paper—we ask everyone we see and receive as many different coordinates. Then at the far end of a darkened cavern there it is: one harassed woman quite surrounded with a crush of petitioners from East and West and carrying on simultaneous Hindi and English conversations as she thumbs through piles of ragged paper, jotting numbers, aimlessly pinning this bundle together and unpinning that.

Behind her, three bureaucrats, presumably her superiors, shuffle other documents on their desks. They have obviously saved every student-concession application ever filed, since nothing else (it turned out) can have been done with them, and all so tattered you'd think they went back to the British except that the paper has disintegrated on ours before it's even submitted. Press of foreigners, terminally impatient, heave forward for attention, receive blank stares, lose impetus, replaced by deluge of Indians infuriated that the aliens seem to be getting more ear. The point is nothing is being done for either, only a lot of gesticulating and pushing. Dinah and Judith prod me forward ("You're so good at this sort of thing") and I do capture enough attention to establish that no cards can possibly be issued for hours, more likely a day. After the announcement that we're leaving tonight and have *ten minutes* to get tickets the clerk gives the impression for a moment that action is impending, disinters a document from the bottom of a stack, tears the corner off, scribbles on it, and hands it over with a mysterious smile: "Return at four." The paper turns out to have written on it, "4." Before I can utter my buts I've been swept aside by a raving-mad Indian who is ready to fling all the papers in the air. The hell with it.

Since the train leaves at seven next morning, it is calculated that our hotel room, booked for twenty-four hours, can sleep us all another night for the price of one. (Why this parsimony in such totally reduced circumstances, heaven knows.) The day is nearly gone in any case—getting everything organized at the V.T. requires filling out forms of the most irrelevant variety. Among the bundles of paper we saw are presumably everybody's ex-applications for train tickets too. To get a ticket you even have to give your age. We stop off at the government tourist office for maps and ideas about a route after Madras which includes a loop around southern India to Coimbatore; then to Dinah's idea of, I suppose, a decompression chamber—the Taj Intercontinental, fully appointed with Hiltonian cool, carpeting, comfort. The address is Nowhere, Everycity, The World. They used to be American oases but now the clientele is Gulf Arab, every man towing several wives deformed by masks, and droves of bored children. You get the impression that Arabs spend a lot of time hanging around hotel lobbies, but it's probably got a hidden purpose somewhere. Of more interest, because it's such a sudden contrast, is the way the Arab men look at us, which reminds me of the way the Indian men don't look at us. As lascivious wild black eyes stroke us head to toe I realize the Indians have no lust in their gaze. If they look at all, which is rare, it is with a plotting or importunate curiosity. Dinah thinks it's because we are below caste and therefore not worth consideration. This seems unlikely to me. Repression? Racism? Something in the diet? Something not in the diet? I lean to that.

One more destination before our own hotel—a certain Dipti's, which Dinah claims sells delicious yogurty drinks. Luckily she can't find it, so we have an excuse for a long walk. The streets are as crowded as those foreshortened Fifth Avenue photographs, but without any particular sense of direction in anyone's eyes. The smell of excrement comes in suffocating clouds in the sticky air. More morale-building signs everywhere: DISCIPLINE MAKES A NATION GREAT, EFFICIENCY SHOULD BE OUR WATCHWORD, WE MARCH TO A BETTER TOMORROW. The shops line the streets like rows of pestilential caves, each one selling some extremely small category of merchandise, from aphrodisiacs to peacock feathers, and the pavements taken up with seated and mobile vendors of plastic toys and things to eat (oranges, of course, the most abundant commodity) and a million customers without the money to buy. The children who are wearing clothes at all favor Bruce Lee T-shirts. Dinah is fretting over finding this drink place and one of the holes eventually reveals itself as Dipti's. Four filthy tables, the others seating Westerners as well, and a selection of "lassis." As we watch they mix yogurt and crushed ice, poison without doubt, with flavors from melon to avocado. A long-haired youth comes in wearing an orange robe, a glazed, introverted smile, and a Bhagwan mala. He and Dinah nod. She is used to encountering allies but doesn't know him. I'm not yet used to that sort of smile.

Back at the hotel, more talk about the ashram. The daily routine will involve five meditations a day during "camp" (ten days of each month). Besides the dynamic and kundalini there is natraj (dancing), humming, and some sort of blue light flashing to stare at. "Aren't there any *quiet* meditations?" I'm daunted by the effort of it all, and what about some good old-fashioned meditative peace? Well, there's a regular Zen group that's quiet, but it goes on *all day long*. Then there is the business, if you're interested in discomforts, of the darshan and the daily discourse, which lasts one and a half to two hours, during which one sits cross-legged on a marble floor. "Agony on the ankles," sighs Dinah. The last bit of anatomy I'd expect. She used to bring a blanket and a cushion with her but now all extras are banned. Something to do with the Great One's allergies—though you're not even allowed to take in your (nonallergenic) blindfold to interpose between stone and anklebone. "Is it essential to be uncomfortable?"

"You have to get into your body."

Dinah even goes to the lectures in *Hindi*, enduring the pain of the posture for the sake of the "meditation" of it. This word is used quite loosely, particularly of anything unpleasant: "Make it a meditation." As for Stuart's "primal"—his current event—it includes not only all the standard five meditations and "screaming your head off" in the intervals, but otherwise maintaining total silence. This is why Dinah is not unhappy herself about joining our southern detour, since his obligatory solitary confinement requires her to vacate their joint bedroom; and her piling in with us, she thinks, might cause frictions. I should think Stuart-as-zombie might cause more. In any case it's clear she is extremely interested in and touchy about our welfare. She really wants us to be happy.

Judith is not; though she is definitely into her body. Her sandals have rubbed raw places, and the pain of her toes tops all concerns but the adjunctive question: When in all this filth will they grow infected?

And I'm not so sure. This may be a permissive, please-yourself religion on one level, but on another it involves a mortification of the flesh related to the Calvinism my family fled. Because it's called another name, are you not supposed to mind? Because it's claimed that what Stuart is going through is a "letting-go"—implying a great release into infinite freedom and relaxation from all constrictions—may one mention, let alone complain, that it's the opposite to me, the most devilish of tortures? But my essential objection is the unfairness of it all: Not only am I unable to find "growth" in pain, but why should Bhagwan be so pampered (is that godlike?) while his devotees suffer? What's worse, the undemocracy of it or the bad manners? Neither, naturally, is supposed to matter.

Somewhere in the same conversation, Judith mentions appositely the matter of Elspeth Waterhouse, the heroine of Dinah's last novel, who burns her skin with cigarettes in order to feel something.

July 29

We start today across the whole of southern India, from the Arabian Sea to the Bay of Bengal. I am so thrilled with the romanticism of it all I hardly mind our having to arrive at 6 A.M., the mandatory early hour for the train, though the ride is twenty-eight hours long enough and the seats clearly numbered and booked. Seats? Actually shelves, seventy-five to a coach in tiers of three. It looks like a prisoner-of-war barracks. Dark, no-watt bulbs and dingy paint, small barred windows you must crouch down in your seat to see through. Apparently not to keep the prisoners in but the beggars out. The train is jammed full long before leaving time. We notice—but are slow to acknowledge the significance of—the rolled-up mattresses the others carry with their baggage. Maybe Indians just carry their beds with them? Why have they brought so much food? Twenty-eight hours? The Indian way to travel?

Off we go. It's an old-fashioned choo-choo with a whistle that propels the train the way horns do cars. The outskirts of Bombay, a single shanty town, go on for hours. Suburban rush-hour trains pass going the other way, so crowded that clusters of people clutch at the doors or cling to the backs of coaches—three or four are killed and more maimed daily, I hear, but this is too common to rate attention. Thicknesses of people mob the tracks beside us when the trains have passed, just as they do the roads, as if all thoroughfares were unfairly limited to the vehicles befitting them. But the alternative is a path that doubles as a sewer. The makeshift huts are never-ending. The stench and mud and despair of it all reminds me of Mexico much more than early postrevolutionary China, where even the worst hovels were brightened with a flower or a bird in a bamboo cage. The only color here is the women's saris: flecks of red, green, or blue so brilliant they look lit from within against the monochromatic mud, rags, dung, decay.

After a while Dinah and Judith fall asleep and, moving down the coach, I find a vacant seat where, with a studied slouch and my bag for a pillow, I can watch the world. The monsoon rain starts up, soon pelting through the windows, but shutting them shuts out the view. Outside there are still people trudging along negotiating the railway ties with care because of the puddles between, some wearing huge green plastic bags slit down one side and tied around the head like Arab headdresses. Others have umbrellas or share plastic sheets. Only one man to be seen in a mac. Underneath, many are dressed like clerks or minor bureaucrats, smartly turned out in clean short-sleeved shirts and white, or at least fresh-looking, trousers—how to achieve that in a shanty town? The little huts are all about six to ten feet across, one hole for a door, put together out of wattle and bits of corrugated tin or flattened kerosene cans, roofs weighed down with stones. But plastic is taking over here, too, and some of them are roofed in it.

The conductor comes by selling meal tickets and I eagerly buy three, but hear the worst about the other question: for some reason only first-class passengers may rent bedding. The conductor is young and springy, more animated than most, and eager to practice his English, of which maybe one word in ten is intelligible unless you have advance knowledge of the subject, when the odds are halved. He speaks five languages, he says, all the main Indian ones except Tamil, and demonstrates on other passengers, some of whom seem to understand him. Whatever it is, it's friendly. Having observed Dinah's outfit he asks, like the epauletted customs lady, if we're connected to "that Rajneesh," and, owning to it, I ask what he thinks about that. "Many people going Rajneesh lecture," he says, "even in *London*. This means something there, something there."

He continues down the passageway with his meal tickets (at the next stop, he explains, he will telegraph to a station ahead for the required number of lunches) and I read the three newspapers I bought at V.T. My companions think I'm queer about newspapers, to care about what's happening in Beirut. Not that this press is too informative. The three papers turn out to contain identical agency stories, hardly edited, even laid out the same way, except for a few local nuggets and some features obviously syndicated from Europe, like one about "psyching yourself out of compulsive overeating," which wouldn't seem to be the central concern of anyone in view.

But we've left people behind at last. The sight as we climb the Western Ghats is not quite assimilable: a prehistoric movie set. Giant cliffs rear up beside us to the right and, across the gorge to the left, waterfalls catapult hundreds of yards down the mountainsides. The track, by way of viaduct and tunnel, is crossing deep ravines and penetrating impossible spurs: the British once knew how to do these things. The conductor beckons me to the door, which he opens for a better view, but only succeeds in drenching us both and the whole inside end of the coach, including a man who had just very carefully washed and dried himself,

with his pocket handkerchief, at the public basin there. Retreat to seat but getting too sore to sit, all imaginable facets
of bottom wearing out. Already? The Indian women plant
themselves cross-legged on the hard wood, and such a posture looks endurable but I can't do it because of my short
skirt. They told me to bring long skirts but never *why*. I
thought it fitted into the general category of orangery and
cultish modesty, therefore to be abjured. It's when you object on principle and are wrong that you really suffer, because you can't even moan. Oh well, only twenty-five hours
to go.

The other passengers display a definite knack for this
whole business. Many have gone straight to sleep on their
lovely bedrolls, the men having removed their trousers
(folded and hung from the luggage rack so that the view
downcoach is of swaying trousers) in exchange for loose
dhotis. The nonsleepers are making friends and a party of
it, squatted on the bunks chatting and joking and eating,
especially at the frequent stations where boys singsonging
"Caw-fee chai, caw-fee chai" pass tiny cups through the
bars, which are spaced just wide enough for them (or a
starved beggar's hand). Betel leaves are favored purchases
too. They chew them for a while and spit the juice, which
looks like blood.

The lunch appears and I wake up Dinah and Judith.
We get large, round covered trays, aluminum and gleaming,
with a compartment each for three chapattis, two rice
cakes, yogurt, lentils, okra, vegetable curry. Delicious,
beautiful, probably lethal. The dishes are collected as the
train pulls out, the seller sprinting to get off as we gain
speed, balancing dishes and trays like a circus juggler. We
drink not, our purifying tablets having failed to melt in the
water before the cups were seized. I am wondering when
this hit-and-run eating is going to make us sick. As it is, the

conversation among us three—in a country where most people must talk a lot about food and how to acquire it—is more usually about constipation and how to get rid of it. But any time now we can presumably expect a dramatic end to that problem. You never know which mouthful will do it. Take this odd fluid, for instance, innocently procured from a man dispensing "caw-fee" in little glasses: with a minute spoon, he collects a few grains of mixed instant coffee and sugar from an old tin and drowns them in hot watered milk from a kettle. The assumption that kettle = boiled = hygienic, quite unsound, is reserved for consideration until after it's gulped down, when one observes the removed glasses being rinsed under the NOT DRINKING WATER! tap at the end of the coach and the spoon being wiped on the seat of the pants.

The rain stops like a lifted curtain as we start across the wide Deccan plateau on top of the mountains. Now and then a tiny village with a temple and a well, children and animals in the river, clay-brick huts. Some of the villages are new, terraces of sensible, simple white cottages with proportionally large porticoes and one room behind. The land isn't used down to the inch as in China, and some of the fields and paddies far surpass others in productivity, but there is a sense of fruitfulness if not luxuriance. But you seldom see anyone working at it. They crouch around in odd pairs or groups, arranged attractively among the greenery and statue-still to watch the train pass by. The men thus posed seem as permanent as the stone slabs that stick up oddly in the fields, resembling gravestones, except the Indians don't bury their dead. Some women are busy, though: in bright saris balancing loads on their heads, usually with a bracing arm, not as clever at it as the Africans, I observe (as if I could do it at all).

The train pulls up for some unseen obstruction and

briefly arrests the attention of three such young girls walking in the field beside the tracks. Their saris are pink, yellow, and turquoise, their skin of smoothest brown set off by silver nose rings, necklaces, earrings, and bracelets, which tinkle as they walk, holding their baskets on their heads. They are shining and fresh as the morning. Ahead of them a bullock with red-lacquered horns lifts his tail, and before the dung has even hit the ground the girls have cupped their long fingers and caught it, put it in their baskets, and veered off the path down to a stream where, unloading their treasure, they pat it neatly into pancakes and lay them out in rows on the rocks to dry in the sun, the last pat leaving an imprint of a hand.

Dinah, having raced through two thrillers she bought at V.T., is mad for other distractions, but finds my window-peering "boring." Such a difference of outlook (inlook?) between us. But we're both hypnotized by the woman opposite brushing her long oiled hair and nimbly plaiting it. She looks entirely Mexican to me, which idiotic perception leads to the idea that Indians, like Mexicans, are mocked by their own past—its monumental legacy among their present squalor, the temples in the villages, remnants of a forgotten brilliance.

Each time we stop, the clammy heat and flies instantly envelop us, and hundreds of vendors cluster to the windows, the more aggressive managing to get inside. We are eating our way across India. It seems necessary to sample everything, bananas, nuts, mangoes, unique-tasting things called dhosas or curd bajis—though as often the more alien substances go out the window again to the beggars. At "Hotgi Junction" appears a man selling coconuts. When we offer to buy, he swipes the top off deftly with a machete, pokes a straw in for us to drink, waits to take it back again to chop into three for the soft meat, and with a fourth flourish even improvises a spoon from a piece of shell—all in seconds.

Still in search of occupation, Dinah finds it in conversation with Judith. They do not address themselves to me, but bits of dialogue stick out and penetrate my tourist trip.

D: "When I first went into psychoanalysis I couldn't have stood groups for anything; and he doesn't seem to take that feeling into account."

J: "At the beginning I felt I wanted to do a group with you, but it doesn't seem important anymore: I feel we've sort of done our groups."

D: "I keep feeling what *are* we doing, going in the wrong direction on this train?"

J: "I must read something of Bhagwan's again; I feel I've been out of touch for ages."

The operative verb is "to feel." I suddenly think of a friend in London who said she never managed to communicate with her husband—or even to avoid interruption—unless she remembered to preface her remarks not with "I think" but "I feel." I have feelings too, you know, I feel like saying, but you get the feeling you can only have them if you're trained to properly recognize them and they're the approved sort. But you can have more words for your feelings and yet not have more feelings. A variety of adjectives available to describe the nuances of your sorrow doesn't deepen it. A worship of that depth does not confer a special place in heaven. But what can I say? My distinct feeling now is of added-on-extra, a freeloading nonfeeler. I find I defer to them in matters of comfort and precedence and it's not important really until the late afternoon, when the violent clogging heat just vanishes with the sun. Not only are they equipped for the temperature drop but they keep having this mumbo-jumbo conversation reminding me of my feelings of, in order of importance, Cold, Nonexistence, and Supreme Irritation. Oh well, they're not too happy either—they wouldn't be stuck here at all if it wasn't for me, poor things. They wanted to come because it sounded exciting, and here they are propped on moving shelves forever. But for me they'd be proper orange pilgrims, safe and soul-searching in Poona. Resentment all round. As for the shelves, I see it is my place to choose an upper for the night, and join six fans and six dim lights upon the ceiling, improvising covers out of my towel and two cotton smocks. For extra warmth Dinah and I pass our half bottle of whiskey up and down and put away enough to have a talk and giggle. The towel and the dresses slither off my bunk at every turn and there is no way to sleep on that hard wood, but at some point the day is over, giving rise to the possibility that the night may eventually end too.

July 30

"CAW-fee, CAW-fee, cawfee, CAW-fee," a nasal twang splits the darkness. Barely see my watch, not quite 5 A.M. Shadowy figure of coffee wallah at the end of my shelf banging his kettle and trampling my fallen towel and smocks. "No," I groan. He is oblivious, leaning farther in and shouting louder. "NO!" "CAW-fee cawfee CAW-fee." "Go *away!*" No effect. No affect? He chants interminably until the whole coach is awake. Only a couple of people buy from him, but nobody can sleep again. Pointless trying anyway. I am acutely, probably incurably bruised from within, weird sensation produced by pressure of bones-on-flesh-on-boards. Having boycotted the coffee, we buy mangoes from the next man along, then a coconut from a one-eyed vendor who manages nonetheless to judge adeptly his machete strokes though a miss could cost him more than an eye.

The light returns as quickly as it left last night. Clear day, red soil, orange lakes, green mountains, blue sky, and much activity now in the fields—peeing and shaving, harvesting and plowing, irrigating and hauling, shepherds leading goats and cows and water buffalo, women laundering at the wells and streams, others water-laden, stone-laden, wood-laden. Clean tidy villages with thatched muffin cottages; perhaps away from the cities the Indian mess is at least diluted. But the next stop by the Krishna Pulverizing Works brings the attendant industrial beggars pleading "Ma! Ma!" from window and aisle. The government asks that they be ignored or they won't stop, sensible advice except in individual cases. Unfortunately they are all individual cases. Just now I am besieged on one side by a little girl who looks my daughter's age and on the other by a boy like my son, if my children had never had enough to eat. Dinah, though peremptorily pukka-toned when issuing orders, is soft-hearted with the beggars. In Poona the thing to do is buy big bunches of bananas, she advises, and dole them out to be sure the money is used in the best way; and she has special friends among the children at the gates, who, when they spot her, chase around the corner where she's free to give to them (as it's "discouraged" at the ashram).

More awake, I reconstruct the whiskey-conversation of the night before. I'm not sure my theories hold up at all well in sobriety. I seem to have held forth on the question of feelings, shortage of, or special compartment for, and related speculations on Englishness. The way the English encapsulate their passions to make them socially acceptable, but as for simply random *feeling*—It Isn't Done. I mean, I said (I think) it's okay to express yourself, even violently, on tree pollarding or the Tory Party or the situation in Taipei, but not your real feelings about your own real life or love or work. In fact I got unhinged on this idea last week at a party and ran amok, scaring people by merely spilling over as I felt, then looking around at the whites of their eyes and wondering (of him and her and him and her), Where do *you* put your passion? There were answers that I even knew for some, but they were always in pockets, respectable, like: Amnesty or Wagner or vintage Jaguars or art critics—categories on behalf of which it was fitting to gesticulate or carry on with eccentric gusto. But for me there's no one to respond to but the odd maniac or New Yorker who shares my jokes and my panics, and I think I've wasted years anesthetizing myself to avoid the pain or ostracism of frightening people with my emotions. Not that sharing an English obsession can't be quite enthralling, like an afternoon spent recently with the world's most passionate expert on how to disrupt motorway hearings, but it requires an amazing eclecticism to cover even a few of their specialties, and you still don't encounter anything very spontaneous. Dinah has always had her writing, as fiery as she was personally chilly, but now I'm wondering if she has chosen to channel her passions out of work and into the very passions themselves—feeling for the sake of it, as approved by Bhagwan. Because of her repressed past, feeling is all.

With Judith it's the other way around. Far from Dinah's upper-class boarding-school straitjacket, she was brought up permissively according to the best nonrepressive socialist precepts—eventually reaching a point where rampages of excessive feeling so overcame her that, rather than express them in that society where we live, she'd hide away as if unclean, locking herself in her tiny flat for a week with a tin of biscuits. Now she has found, after years of putting the pieces together, a set of intellectualizations for her feelings; her spirit finds organization in the words of Freud to Laing to Reich to Lacan to Gurdjieff to Bhagwan. So she and Dinah end up in a similar pocket though starting from opposite ends.

The result is the same for me: I can talk to them, though not to many of the English. (I am after all both English and American, and therefore, in a way, neither.) "I love you with my English self" became my drunken incantation, but it's incomplete—naming friends they've met with whom I feel really free, all Americans and other "foreigners." Dinah, justifiably miffed by this (why am I toying with this friendship? because I know it's finished?) and certainly my alcoholic match at this point, ridiculed this split: "Take Anna Magnani," she pointed out a passionate exemplar (who isn't remotely related to my view of myself except as I'd just wildly misrepresented it). "I should think Anna Magnani is Anna Magnani *all* the time." Got me there.

No more heavy talks today. Wallow in the rhythm of the ride, clickety clack chuffety chuff too-oot too-ooot. Somewhere in the night we passed the border of the state of Tamil Nadu and the railway signs are now in the Tamil alphabet (as well as the Latin). I take to jotting down the station names I like. Renigunta, Puttur, Ponpadi, Tiruttani, Basin Bridge Junction, Pattabviam. MADRAS.

The first trick in Madras is to organize a way out of it. Since we're at the station we decide to book tickets ahead to my leaf-protein place, Coimbatore. This is not a straightforward affair, although it appears to involve nothing more serious than a slight delay since the operative ticket window is closed for lunch. Forming a queue of three, we are soon surrounded by beggars. Some of them are obviously families and in residence. An old man with paralyzed legs hauls himself about nudging and rubbing at us like a hungry cat, and ragged urchins plead with multiple pluckings and horrendous eyes. There are too many of them to give any one of them something, so we distract ourselves with theatrical busy-ness and talk. After filling out our ticket application forms so Madras will know that Dinah is forty, I am thirty-nine, and Judith thirty-two, Judith and I wait while Dinah enterprisingly goes off to phone for a room at a hotel at Mahabalipuram, a seaside spot with famous rock temples down the coast. To avoid acknowledging the pathetic entreaties of a midget amputee I focus on a sign above the window, decorated in death's heads. BEWARE OF CHEATS, it reads. DO NOT SHOW YOUR TICKETS TO ANYONE EXCEPT RAILWAY STAFF IN UNIFORM. THERE HAVE BEEN CASES OF SUBSTITUTION OF LONG DISTANCE BY SHORT DISTANCE TICKETS, BY CHEATS.

Dinah returns with magazines, books, things to eat—all purchased in a vain effort to obtain a fifty-paisa piece for the phone call; this coin appears to be nearly obsolete. Unable to eat the dubious speckled mush she's found for us, we lay it in its banana-leaf wrapper on a nearby ticket-windowsill. In an instant a little girl has snatched it. The paralyzed old man, furious at missing out (he couldn't have reached it anyway) starts haranguing her, but others intervene in her defense and while the row continues, she retreats with the prize back to her family a few yards away. There on the mat which is their home they share it out, father, mother, baby, two larger children. Their address: Under the Train Departure Sign, Madras Station, Tamil Nadu, India.

When eventually our ticket window opens we are told, despite its clear designation COIMBATORE (each window handles a different set of destinations painted in permanent white on the wood, together with its own opening and closing times), that it is the wrong window. The dialogue disclosing this takes longer than usual since the other end of it is so patently unbelievable. Three more tries—two of which involve a different lunch hour which has only just begun—and we successfully acquire some tickets; but another hour's gone before we've succeeded in checking our bags at the Left Luggage, because the right people and forms (two of each) cannot be found. Never mind, at last Dinah has got the coin for the phone and has managed even to get through. And the day isn't quite over—three hours remain to devote to Madras before we must catch the last bus for Mahabalipuram.

A little sightseeing. The guidebook recommends the banyan tree at the Theosophical Society and a certain temple. We satisfy two of the hundreds of porters, beggars, and drivers who badger us, choosing a couple of bicycle-rickshaw boys who pedal frantically through the traffic toward the unknown, since they don't understand us. Although English is supposed to be India's lingua franca, few of those born postraj can speak it, and these drivers have to be young to do the work. Youth is all they've got: They are made of bone and sinew and propelled by betel juice, their teeth stained red and black from it, and are obviously seriously malnourished. One has a swollen arm and trouble keeping up: what possible future? It's almost impossible to focus on the fact that we are doing them a favor. And we are so blatantly anachronistic that we draw an audience at every pause. The guilt of passing the poor on the muscles of the poor needs only a hill and the view of our driver's inhuman distress to make our progress nearly unendurable.

They deposit us outside a temple—which temple, or

whether it's the recommended one, doesn't seem to matter. A "guide" presents himself among the milling petitioners at the gate and, since he masterfully sweeps us past the others, we submit to his care. Within minutes he has relieved us of ten rupees for an "offering" he claims is obligatory, consisting of a coconut for each of us in a basket of blossoms and bananas; led us to an altar where he dramatically smashes our nuts while fending off the hungry women and children clawing for the pieces; made a few incomprehensible observations about the brilliant ceramic figures of gods and animals that decorate the roof; and demanded an enormous fee. We settle for a sum that makes everyone unhappy and drive off leaving a disgruntled mob glowering behind us.

A particular problem of our group is its number. One can move, two can confer, even four might have a policy or a spokesperson, but when there are three, one can be peeled off or another swept along in a confusion as if agreement somehow had been reached with the other two. Nothing in India relates to ordinary sensations of generosity or miserliness—for one thing, if you give there is no end to it, only the request for more. When you hand a child a banana it's not just that all his friends want bananas too but that he wants *another* banana. Why not? Why expect him to go away as if he's not still starving? Worse, why expect gratitude, token thanks at least, a nod, recognition? With poverty so catastrophic, what do such gestures mean? But what is there to do about it? I remember hearing James Baldwin speak in New York years ago, lashing out at a white liberal audience, one of whom stood and said: "I feel terrible about your oppression, but why should *I* be made to feel guilty? It's not *my* fault." And Baldwin replied "No, it's not your fault that I am black and you are white and these attitudes exist. *But it's not my fault either.*"

Somehow or other—maybe it's the intervention of a

coffee vendor, but I suspect it's Dinah's unusual miming of a banyan tree—the rickshaw wallahs find the Theosophical Society, lair of the late Annie Besant and her protegé Krishnamurti. A wistful young man is at our heels at once offering to show us around. When we emphatically refuse, he meekly responds that he wants no money. But "of course they all say that," says Dinah. We have to put up with him anyway as he won't go away.

The gardens, quiet, scented, full of peace and birdsong, make you realize how luscious it all could be, given the means. As for the Banyan tree, "second biggest in India," is it a tree? or a mother with masses of offspring and uncut umbilical cords? I'm filled with unanswered questions about the genesis of this place and Krishnamurti, who Dinah reveals is the only other living man whom Bhagwan regards as an enlightened master. In our attempts to elude our guide there is no time for pausing, though. Have to be satisfied with a portrait of Madame Blavatsky (who founded theosophy in the nineteenth century) purchased at the Madame Blavatsky portrait stall.

The wistful young guide leads us back to our rickshaws and actually wants no money. The amazing sensation this produces is soon dispelled by the rickshaw wallahs' drawing to a premature halt in some deserted nowhere and demanding one hundred rupees (twelve dollars) to advance. Discussion makes them forget what English they'd mustered for the initial demand; nothing is understood but the number one hundred. What to do? We hand over fifty, which according to Dinah's calculations of Poona prices is at least twice the usual annual wage, and they respond with a go-slow, dismounting and pushing at creeping pace. We pass a sign saying, of all things, DELAY BREEDS CORRUPTION. At this rate we'll miss our bus. Impasse. However, the elements intervene with a sudden colossal monsoon downpour. The boys, already soaked with sweat, conscientiously raise the fringed hoods of the rickshaws so that bits of us, though none of them, are protected; when it's over they proceed normally, if grimly, to the station. Once delivered we are still unnerved enough to ask at a rickshaw information booth what the correct fee should have been. Of the crowd that gathers, no one is willing to snitch, but when it's revealed what in fact we paid, there are uniform sniggers and nods of satisfaction: "Too *much!*"

Of course we have missed the last tourist bus to Mahabalipuram anyway, but the hotelier told Dinah on the phone that it was only forty minutes on the regular bus. More harassments to come: the porter we hire—or who more accurately seizes our bags and won't relinquish them except to a friend, a frail old fellow who actually gets to do the heaving while his sturdier cohort employs his strength to dun us and issue instructions—demands ten rupees per bag. Since the normal rate is one rupee we offer two, but they will neither accept it nor go away. Dinah does her English schoolmistress imitation, Anna-to-the-King-of-Siam, articulating loudly and with a tried patience as if her interlocutor were deaf or a very small brat. It's obviously the sort of stuff that made the raj go round, but cuts no ice now. After we've got our bags back we ignore them, the policy of last resort, until they accept the merely double payment.

No sooner are we seated on the bus than a hand is thrust through the slats of the seat ahead with a wail: "Alma, alma." It's a woman with a nursing baby; feeling misunderstood she changes her chant to "Money, money." It would be easier to ignore her too if only there were a distraction, such as the bus moving off, but nothing moves except trays of more-or-less edible merchandise, which no one can afford, up and down the aisle. The baby gazes at us over his mother's shoulder and she yanks him down in misplaced irritation; next time he looks at us she slaps him. We take surreptitious snorts of whiskey (Tamil Nadu is a dry state) to keep up what's left of the spirits with ditto, and finally, more than an hour later, we're off. The rain resumes. Flaps of cloth held up with string bows on the windows are let down to keep the wet out and we can't see the view; it's soon too dark anyway. The bus, already jammed, stops often and more people pile in. Most of them are presumably going home after the day's work, but some are wearing flowers and fresh red spots on their third eyes and traveling with their children, having attended a festival in honor of today's god.

In the dark Dinah tells us something about the Theosophical Society. I had noticed its insignia, a combined cross and star of David topped by a swastika: Madame Blavatsky's idea had been to combine the best of all religions (the swastika emblematic of the Hindu) into a philosophy of universal brotherhood. Her most interesting follower was Annie Besant, an early feminist and radical who, in the course of her conversion to India mysticism, had recognized the New Messiah in the infant Krishnamurti, and acquired him from his parents to be trained and cosseted according to his station in the house and Botanic Garden we had seen. Apparently there was trouble with the parents later; in their efforts to reclaim their son they took Mrs. Besant to court which, being British (in the view of many), sided against them and with Krishnamurti's Caucasian protector. The child was brought up surrounded with advisers in enlightenment, did what was expected of him, and at his twenty-first birthday Theosophists assembled from around the world to hear "the new world teacher" finally speak. No one was prepared for what followed: a denunciation of not only their training but their expectations of him. He was no more enlightened, he announced, than anyone else, and he was leaving them to become a pilgrim. An old man now, he has never gone back on his repudiation of his origins, and yet has acquired a wide following of his own. People flock to hear him on his regular international tours, and among the mystical cognoscenti he is much revered. Mrs. Besant never recovered from her disappointment, however, and died in 1933.

The aisles of our bus are soon spilling over with limbs and scrawny bottoms and we obviously must share our bench. When a woman carrying a sleeping baby and towing a small boy squeezes along, we push in for her. The boy has pustulating eyes which he keeps mopping with a filthy handkerchief. The mother tries to keep the three of them propped up in their bit of seat without letting the whimpering boy fall asleep, probably because they haven't far to go. She is clearly exhausted herself, and in a bad time (if there ever was a good): the holes in her nose and ears are ringless. The boy's eyes are unspeakable, surely he is going blind, and he keeps wiping his oozy hands on Judith's skirt. I think I would shrink away but Judith leans instead to Dinah, who is banker, and asks for one hundred rupees for the mother to take the boy to a doctor. As the trio struggle to leave through the crowd, Judith thrusts the money in the mother's hand and mimes her intention. In awe and surprise the woman thanks her. Gratitude is expensive. Dinah predicts in my ear, "Now she'll take him off on all the other buses to beg from tourists." But there aren't enough tourists this time of year, I reassure myself, even if there's enough cynicism anytime.

This forty-minute ride has so far taken two hours. It seems improbable that we are on the right bus, or that the conductor has understood where we want to go, or that it can be found in such a blackness anyway, even if the windows weren't all covered over. The other passengers are gone. A dream: You are on a bus, they say it's India but there are no flags, we are only going and it's always night.

And then the conductor tells us we are here; indeed there is a lit-up sign, SILVERSANDS. We're dumped: now what? A long sandy trail, no moon. We feel our way until some distant lights suggest a destination. It materializes: a collection of thatched cottages quite unlike the native efforts, fanciful and winged. We might as well be in the Caribbean, or trapped in a trendy martini commercial. The reception hall, a larger thatched affair, advertises ROOMS FOR SWINGERS and BEACH COMBERS CLUB and "Hot news! Monthly moonlit get togethers!" Eh? We are shown to a cottage down silent, sandy paths by several young men, one of whom unlocks the door and heads straight for a gramophone where he starts to play a Crosby, Stills and Nash record. In this allegedly dry state there is a bar and fridge containing setups. The lights have dimmers and are snared in little baskets. The place has no substance. Is it a stage set? Hanging around, the young men look at us, follow us—anxious for our approval? Awaiting instructions? Digging the swingers? Since we can't get rid of them we go outside again; abruptly they lead us through more sand across an outdoor dance floor, past a sign in Russian reading PECTOPAH to the dining hall, another thatched roof held up on poles with cooking going on at the far end—dark, open to the beach, sand floor, no customers. A grin attached to a shadow looms out of the night with its hand sticking out: "Hi! I'm Michael! I'm the manager of this hotel!" and seconds on an even heartier, gargantuan voice booms, "Hi! I'm Yash! I'm the owner of his hotel!" Well. They sit with us during dinner—the dim light reveals them both as pale-skinned, upper-caste—making feverish conversation, as if terminating a life's vow of silence. We are constantly solicited for our opinion of the place. The Rus-

sians love it and send tour groups, says Yash, though lately
have begun to complain about the lizards and are deserting
him for a new hotel down the beach with ordinary old
walls. "But don't you think it's pretty? What's a lizard here
or there? Don't you love it?"

Dinah, tactfully suggesting that we'd anticipated something rather simpler—a native hostelry or a cabin—is led as
we follow to a veritable extravaganza of a cottage with not
only the bar and fridge but a plush two-seater swing hanging from the rafters. "For swingers," says Yash, pushing off.
"Get it?" He is doubled up with pleasure at the arrangements. "I designed it all myself." A cunning spotlight shows
his face gleaming with nervous sweat; the ropes of the swing
strain to hold his bulk. "Carolina Moon" is coming from
the stereo. I notice several lizards of varied sizes and colors
eying us from the straw surrounds. "Aren't they cute?" says
Yash. "They wouldn't hurt a fly. Well of course that's all
they *would* hurt." The young men pause to guffaw appreci-
atively as they dash to retrieve our bags from the original
cottage. Yash, who disappears as well to arrange for some
drinks on the house, returns squeezed into a swimsuit. A
midnight dip is definitely vetoed, but they'll settle for a
dance. Dinah accepts. Exchanging a horrified glance, Judith and I retreat to the bedroom, but find ourselves tailed by
our rejected dance partners. They want to show us the air-
conditioning switch. The bathroom! I think, finding it, but
am relentlessly pursued for a demonstration of the plumbing. There is no alternative but to return to our jocular
host, swallow the drinks, and plead exhaustion. Like lambs
they say good night and retreat. We've been so alert for
predators after a day of nothing else that their motives
seemed wholly sinister. But maybe they're just lonely?

July 31

Whoever else is lonely, we're not about to be. They wake us in the morning and sit with us at breakfast, summoning the resident snake charmer for cabaret ("Don't give him anything, just buy one of his flutes"), follow us resolutely and silently through the sand, and the only successful evasive tactic is to leave the premises altogether. By daylight the hotel turns out to be directly on the Bay of Bengal, deserted to the horizon. We leave our Eastern neo-Western fantasy paradise for the two-hour walk to the temple silhouetted against the farthest bit of sky. This beach is too unlikely, too perfectly untouched to believe. A place that anywhere else would be jammed in July is the only totally unpopulated piece of India. It contains nothing but elaborate shells (some still inhabited) on fine white powder next to lapping azure waves. Not even sea-glass because no Coke bottles have ever broken here to be washed back; no plastic, no beer cans, cigarette ends, contraceptives, oil, chewing gum, picnic garbage, burned-out bonfires, footprints. Just God's beach, original design. It's the sort of thing you've got to see to realize you've never seen it.

We spend the afternoon among the temples—friezes,

statues, carvings in high relief out of the solid rock, exuberant representations of the myths of the gods, chariots, and elephants and whimsical beasts. Nobody importunes us; the people are obviously prospering from the tourists they attract (more Indian than foreign: the temples are a special Hindu mecca) and those who offer wares or services will actually take no (at any rate No-No-No) for an answer. On an ancient lighthouse above the town we watch a family of wild monkeys. Some boys below are teasing them with stones, and Father Monkey is showing off to his two wives (each with a baby clinging to her underside) and adolescent children, making daringly provocative forays in and out of stones' range, challenging the boys with cackles and silly leaps while the family sensibly makes for the less accessible heights. I've never seen zoo animals in their own place; it seems more special than the greatest rock-hewn temple. Not only monkeys: later we look up suddenly to half a skyful of green parrots. What next, tigers?

Only the lovely lonely beach. The sun doesn't set so much as dive into the dunes, and walking home we lose sight of one another in the moonless dark, guided by phosphorescent waves. To find such stillness in the crowd of India.

Back among the swingers we are intercepted at the door of our cottage by Yash, brightly wrapped in red sarong with white sea-horse appliqué, inviting us to a barbecue in honor of a coachload of American schoolteachers. Other boarders have turned up. The snake charmer is on show with lady assistant this time, supplementing cobras with inaudible magic and the sale of flutes, before a banquet on the sands. A Mughal meal of flesh and fowl and fish (among it all, wouldn't you know, was the fatal mouthful). The schoolteachers, after weeks of travel in less bountiful circumstances, are in good appetite, and pleased to see new people as they've tired of discussing their mutual digestive tracts, all, one gathers, that they've found they have in common. An American cross section—token black, token Jew, token Oriental, even token nun. The nun has her hair in curlers all evening. I can't get over seeing a nun with her hair in curlers, but Judith and Dinah do not find it noteworthy. The meal, never actually concluded, drifts apart as Manager Michael leads the diners off crabbing—one of the young men picks them out with torchlight, others leap in the air and down among the waves for their prey, a mob of wettening teachers in pursuit. Dinah, who tries anything once, is determinedly off to catch her own crab; Judith disappears; and I lie down on the beach with my toes in the Bay of Bengal. What I can't work out is the sky: the constellations are different. A new sky! Eventually I locate Cassiopeia way down on the northern horizon; nothing else is familiar.

August 1

I've been waiting to get sick; here we go. Montezuma's revenge, gyppy tummy, what's the name in India? Delhi belly, I am informed. Agony, anyway. Bands of bright pain seize me around the middle, fade out, return. Unfortunately we have to travel at noon, though Laing's Lomotil will stop peristalsis so I won't have to hold up the bus every few minutes. But it makes the pain worse by containing it.

Before we leave Dinah and Judith—who are fine—ride the waves in a catamaran, and I, clutching my stomach, hang around enviously on the beach watching both them and the progress of a contraption devised by Yash's brother —a sort of stationary Mississippi paddle boat meant to generate power from waves—which is being assembled and bashed into the sand by dark-skinned workers in loincloths chanting the local version of "Yo Heave Ho." I'll never know if it worked.

Yash has arranged a free ride for himself and us on the teachers' bus to Madras so that we can make our night train to Coimbatore. When told about my bone-bruising on the train he kindly produces an old bedspread for cushion and comfort. It is christened Yashmat. In Madras with several hours to spare, we accept his invitation to the movies. His family owns a huge cinema showing three films at once. We choose "A Lyrical Love Story of Two Innocent Hearts" called *Geet Gaata Chal*, which is so packed we have to sit on our suitcases in the back. Since I am regularly passing out with spasms of pain, I'm provided with an even more simplified view of an already rather rudimentary plot: a foundling minstrel boy in an idyllic, timeless, rural India, meets spoiled upper-caste girl and, after all conceivable reversals, joins her in a chaste embrace (not, naturally, before the revelation that his lineage matches hers). Every scene more lusciously romantic than the last, every lady pinker and man jowlier than any seen Indian (with the possible exception of our host), no hint of poverty, malnutrition, forms to fill in: a perfect three-hour holiday from life out there. Six million Indians a day attend films; it is their only escape.

After "tiffin" in a restaurant which has forgotten which

world it's in, we're back on the train for the night. Its discomforts, somewhat alleviated by the Yashmat, are on the other hand aggravated by the state of my interior. I'm awake all night in a state of febrile argument with Shree Rajneesh (as if he's answering).

From what I've heard about your ashram, while it appears to be founded on the search for self in freedom and love as opposed to hair-shirted asceticism, there seems to be a great impulse toward self-flagellation. Part of it is in the structure of some of the meditations and exercises (to induce feeling? through pain?) and part through the weird lengths to which your followers must go on account of your physical deficiencies (after all those lives?). Dinah has us obsessed with the scent of our hair. I can't believe that all this scrutiny by nose has much point, since you yourself are unlikely to be poking your schnozz into our skulls; and why must we be bitten to bits by mosquitoes because you dislike the smell of repellent? Is that nice? As for me, "doing my thing" is writing; yet you don't let anybody take notes. Why? Dinah says it's all transcribed and produced into books: Are we meant not to compete with the tape recorder? Why must we participate in these diabolical "meditations"? Put up with such discomfort? I resent receiving a message and a reality so in opposition to each other. Maybe no one else does; they come for other reasons, converts in advance, whereas doubters obviously stay at home.

And what do you do with the follower problem? There's Laing, whose partisans are a bunch of professional ("amateur" corrects one of them) maniacs, exotifying their craziness for the attention or even applause it earns, until it becomes a parody of itself. There's Ivan Illich who, having written in *Deschooling Society* about the need to dissolve schools and to promote the freedom to learn when and what one wants and needs to learn, let his disciples set up a school in Mexico which grew to resemble a fortress, with barbed wire and guards and fifty-dollar laminated photo passes necessary for admittance. Beyond parody to contradiction. There are all those Fidelistas who, in the name of their leader's direct approach to people and government, have constructed one of the world's least penetrable bureaucracies. I know Dinah says you claim to know what's going on in your name all over the ashram: then how can you fail to stem that sycophantic slop that people write about you on the back page of the newsletter, so in contrast to your own words? and decorate it with all those photographs of you in flattering hats—graven images cosmeticized? How come you let this hair-wash nonsense be an instrument of torment? *What about the beggars?*

We're going to Coimbatore to see the mechanical cow in operation, a possible answer to all those half-lives out there, the people who have never had a proper meal, a roof, a chance. Three-quarters of the population is starving, I have read. Millions of people haven't even got a "hutment." There will be a billion Indians by the year 2000. Your scheme of things is just an insult in this setting—one of those luxuries, like psychoanalysis, which presents itself every so often as a faddish answer to Western metaphysical dissatisfaction in the face of plenty, but a really vicious joke in India. I always think in this context of my journalist father's garden in Cuernavaca, where he lives in exile having been deported from America to England in the fifties. People of the Old Left come to visit, sit behind the walls (which screen out poverty as bad as this), and when they find the weather always glorious, the daiquiris flowing, the swimming pool heated, the food exciting to the most exhausted palate, the trees going so far as to bear fruit and flowers at once—they start to fail and falter, then to wonder—with all their needs and wants so perfectly met, why are they still miserable? Their personal difficulties were habitually masked by complaint about life's trivial mechanics, or the political situation, or the weather, or inflation. Now with nothing tangible in the world to worry about they have to confront the sources of their real unhappiness. You'd have a lot to say to them. No one's as miserable as the truly sated. But what has it to do with *your* countrymen? I have not seen this question answered, even addressed. To me it's the important question.

Bill Pirie wouldn't have five minutes for you (although he's certainly not intolerant of some of your ilk: I heard him say about Taoists, "What a nice lot of people! How sensible!")—but he hasn't really any time at all because he's talking about survival. You might say his interest is more fundamental in that he is indirectly preparing people for such spiritual quests. Though I'm sure he'd roar at such a notion. But surely his work comes first? Being Here Now takes on fresh meaning when you think of it in terms of starving. It's as in China in 1957 when people said to me, "What good is political democracy to people with nothing to eat? What is freedom of the press to people who can't read?"

So here we have on one side Bill Pirie, isolated hero in an actual position to help mankind, and on the other You, appealing to selfishness over altruism in the matter of the rich seeker's personal enlightenment, peace of mind, samadhi, whatever you call it. One could think of you both on the track of the problem: What the World Wants. But Pirie is talking about Want as Need, and you—Want as Desire.

August 2

I suppose there was a little sleep, but dreams continued where semiconsciousness left off. "I don't want to go to the moon" are the first words to surface: "Count me out of your moon trip." It's morning and Coimbatore. I'm feeling really sick. A telegram was sent to a Dr. Kamalanathan at the Home Science College, but there was no way of receiving an answer—so whether they expect us isn't known. Too early to ring, so we park ourselves in the Ladies Waiting Room to wait for a decent hour. Many women come and go, take a shower, wash their children, wrap themselves in fresh saris. Cleaners (male) barge in frequently but either they find us, or think themselves, invisible—eyes averted but for obstacles to brooms. If the obstacle is human, it is tapped to move. They sweep under our chairs, mop, and return for another sweep within the hour.

We read each other stories from the papers. Today's *Express* contains two items of interest:

ROTARY OFFER OF ARTIFICIAL LIMB

Karaikal, Aug. 1—An artificial limb, pertaining to right leg of a man, is ready to be donated to any disabled person in need of it and who approaches the Karaikal Rotary Club, according to Mr. D. Paulraj, newly installed president of the club.

In the adjoining column, a story with local origins:

PATRICIDE BY HERMAPHRODITE

Coimbatore, Aug. 1—A hermaphrodite allegedly killed her or his father, for the latter's failure to arrange for her or his wedding.

Twenty-five-year old Kamakshi was born as "she" to a handloom weaver but for the past seven years she became "he" with the development of secondary male sex characteristics. This posed a problem for the father Karunayappa Mudaliar. When Kamakshi pressed her or his father to arrange for marriage, he excused himself saying that he had no money. Yet recently, he performed the marriage of his youngest daughter Rasakka (17). This provoked Kamakshi to demand that "he" must be married to a "girl." When the father expressed inability to do, Kamakshi allegedly whipped up an arubal and cut his or her father in the leg on July 29. The father died next day.

At 8 A.M. it seems possible to ring the Home Science College: I limp painfully to the phone to hear that Dr. Kamalanathan is expected at nine. Walking around a bit, with frequent side trips back to the Ladies Waiting Room, helps divert attention from the stomach. OUR PLEDGE SERVICE WITH SMILE says a sign. Rows of other notices along the platform indicate NON-VEGETARIAN REFRESHMENT ROOM, RETIRING ROOMS (UPSTAIRS), UPPER CLASS WAITING ROOM GENTS and, as in every station we've passed,

HIGGINBOTHAM'S BOOKSELLERS LTD. Whatever happened to Higginbotham, an insufficiently diversionary question if ever there was one.

On the other hand, it is interesting to note that the sullen beggars have disappeared. The station produces not one importunity, and no one appears to sleep, live, or scavenge here. It is all faded grandeur, an impossible survivor of Victoria's India. After our train there is another, and suddenly as it pulls in, the platform is thick with raucous, jabbering vendors with sweet tea and pancakes, and a convulsion of porters (red turbaned, diapered) who to a man vanish as the train leaves. Higginbotham's closes. Only the cleaner in the waiting room sweeps on.

At nine-fifteen I ring again. "Dr. Kamalanathan is in prayer for an hour." OUR PLEDGE COURTESY AND CUSTOMER'S SATISFACTION. FOR COMPLAINTS ABOUT CORRUPTION PLEASE CONTACT DPTY. CHIEF VIGILANCE OFFICER TEL. NO. 35743 (MADRAS). I wish I could go to bed.

Finally Dr. K. is there, solicitous and welcoming. Take a taxi, she directs, and mind not to pay more than five rupees. The taxi driver demands ten, of course; but we have arrived.

Dr. Kamalanathan, a warm, bustling woman of obvious energy and competence, greets us with what becomes a refrain for the next two days: What a pity that her senior colleague Dr. Devadas is away! Now *there* is a woman of such intellect and vigor, how can another possibly fill in? (Dr. Devadas becomes a mythic superhuman who needs no sleep, writes a learned paper a day, and attends one international conference a week, the world's greatest expert in forty-two fields and as many languages. Also she is married to a policeman.) No flies on Dr. K. either. She leads us directly across a large space surrounded with school buildings and filled with flocks of girls in many-colored saris to the leaf-protein extractor, discussing the project with more knowledge of the facts than I have questions.

The machine, painted green to match the violent leafy smell it exudes, is being operated in a shed behind the main buildings by other beautifully saried young women. (Bill Pirie: "Until it was the women who took up leaf protein in India, they just produced muck. The women have standards.") Beyond on the wall a chart outlines the process:

1. Wash leaves
2. Chop
3. Pulp
4. Press and strain
5. Coagulate and filter
6. Press and preserve

Drooling bile-colored liquid, the machine masticates the leaves, stems and all, into a mush which is belted along, juice pumped to a steaming U tube where it is curdled and filtered through nylon stockings, pressed and air dried in an oven. One hundred kilograms of alfalfa produces an average of one and a half kilograms of protein concentrate, which is then made into laddu, moist sweet cakes, for distribution among the small children of a village nearby. They had to devise a new food and make it a special treat: "If we put it in a known recipe they complain about the color." Children in five other villages are fed different supplements as controls, three with an alternative protein (skim milk, horsegram [an herb cultivated for fodder, the seeds being used as food], or vegetable protein), one with a nonprotein caloric supplement (tapioca), and one the basal diet only; and all 360 children are measured regularly for height and weight gain. The cost of the leaf protein, even on this experimental level, is a fifth that of meat. Has the machine ever gone wrong? No problems in a year of operation, but they are fifteen days ahead with stocks just in case. The nightmare is the breakdown of a major part which might need an imported replacement, with all that red tape. It took a year to get the original machine in. But it is obviously pampered, and "when Dr. Pirie comes," Dr. K. says, "he spends eighteen out of twenty-four hours with his machine." Its fiber by-product is used at the school as well, as cattle fodder. Dr. K. shows us a dozen cows, the first traditional-looking specimens, as opposed to ambulatory skeletons, I've seen in India, and the garden where the school's trying experimental plants; other women join and leave us as we walk, and all of them seem—after the days we've spent window-shopping on poverty from the trains—as unlikely as their cows, concerned, bright, nourished, proud, pleased with life. With their fine bones, graceful hands, and doll-like way of tipping the head to say yes, they make me feel grotesquely clumsy, an outdated model that ought to have been discarded long ago by evolution.

Dr. K. shows us the nursery school (the college starts young, though it is mostly the equivalent of secondary school), which is decorated with pictures of lakes and waves. The teacher explains, "This week we enlighten them on water."

I am still needing a stomach transplant and plead finally to sit down. In the feminine atmosphere the talk is about women. Dr. K. mentions "how recently in Tamil Nadu we had full rights." The "recently," which puzzles us, turns out to be fifteen centuries ago, when women "lost the franchise and could no longer choose their husbands." This measure of time seems incomprehensible to a Westerner; perhaps it is comforting to encompass such eons in one's view of events—a mere lifetime, then, is too meaningless a span to produce unreal expectations of change. She continues to outline their history as if matters of millennia could be gossiped about like yesterday's leaf-protein menu: "It got bad for us after the Muslim invasion [in the thirteenth to fourteenth centuries] but the low point was probably the nineteenth century under the British." What about suttee—the practice of wives cremating themselves alive along with their husbands? Aryan or later. It started in Rajasthan when a very beautiful young warrior died and his wife, "preferring death to dishonor," threw herself passionately on his pyre. But what's dishonorable about widowhood? "Remarriage is very rare and widows are often taken advantage of." (Later I read in Mulk Raj Anand's *Seven Summers* of a character whose liberal ideas were demonstrable by virtue of his membership in "a society which stood for widow remarriage, the abolition of caste, the raising of the age of consent, etc.") Girls are married off very young because "girls aren't raped after they wear the tali" (she points out her toe ring, the Hindu wedding ring). "Men look at your feet first, to see if you are married." She also shows us a gold amulet around her neck shaped like a tiger's tooth. In the old days the man had to kill the tiger and bring his bride a real tooth.

While we're presuming to discuss her ornaments I ask about the spot on her forehead. It's called kumkum, she says, and is auspiciously worn on the third eye. Wives also sometimes daub their hair-partings with color, but widows use neither: kumkum is "to bless your husband" (not yourself).

Marriage is a constant preoccupation at the Home Science College, but not for the usual reasons. Ironically, it is a *sine qua non* for women wishing independence. The pursuit of an academic or scientific career is virtually impossible for a single woman because she is prohibited freedom of movement. Most marriages are still arranged by the families (according to the horoscope of each), but once they are married they are magically liberated, even to study abroad alone. Dr. K. herself got her master's degree at Cornell on a Fulbright, taking a year off on her own after the birth of her daughter. It's getting better, but not at much of a rate. Dowries are illegal now—"they used to be given to the father of the groom for him to squander"—though the custom continues because of atavistic ideas the law can't reach. Future sons-in-law expect a minimum of bike, watch, and radio; but it can be far worse, with payoffs required to all the groom's relatives, who, if dissatisfied, can drive young brides to suicide. Still, she insists, there is progress. The main thing is the general attitude: "Gandhiji changed so many concepts that affected us. He said *to be yourself.*"

"Gandhiji" (the affectionate term: "Gandhi" is never used) figures large at the Home Science College (twin to an equivalent male institution established thirty years earlier). Sri Avinashilingam, the school's founder, who continues to turn up daily although quite old now, is mentioned often with respect and reverence; and he seemingly never is referred to at all without the subclause, "He is a bachelor, you know." The significance of this, or the emphasis on it, eludes us until we realize that they mean he took a Gandhi-inspired vow of brahmacharya (celibacy), which alone seems to elevate one to an awe-inspiring status. Whether he tests himself, as the Mahatma did, by sleeping with but resisting fresh young girls each night, is not mentioned; but I can't help remembering Bill Pirie telling me that Avinashilingam means "the indefatigable penis." ("Mind you," he qualified, "lingam now has a rather broader significance than mere penis. You know those domes in the temples they anoint with ghee. It's a celestial penis of some sort.") The point is that "Our Founder" has dedicated himself to Gandhiji's principles, a simple life devoted to India and Indians, despite his origins in "the richest family in the district." "He lives in a student's room!"

Some of this information is later repeated by the only

male teacher, a Mr. Narayanswamy, who possesses a hypnotically white set of teeth, white Gandhian shirt, and white third eye. We are assigned to him after lunch for "further illumination." Judith is fed up and retires instead to one of the hostel rooms—presumably similar to Our Founder's—which we've been given for the night. This man surrounded by three thousand women speaks generously about his colleagues and students. "There is no difference between a man and a woman, I would say," Mr. Narayanswamy tells us with his constant gleaming grin, then ruins it: "or for that matter between a man and a monkey, or a man and a dog." Women do need strict discipline of course. They are not permitted to leave the college, for example, even those over twenty. "In our country women do not move out lonely," he explains. But he himself is certainly not overwhelmed, if outnumbered—"Oh no, you see I don't see *women*, I see them all as *disciples*." I am reminded of the unendearing phrase one constantly hears in Russia: "He's a Jew, but . . ."

Not only Judith but Dinah is starting to feel a bit daunted. On the way back to our room she produces an audible shudder. "Too much virtue," she defines her complaint. "What's wrong with virtue?" "It's the good *works*," she mumbles. "Ugh. And it's all so *tidy*. You know me, I'm for exploration of the self. Good old shambles and chaos."

The school does have the air of a mission—bells and devotion to duty, simplicity, modesty, probity, cleanliness, holiness—with the added flavor of Gandhian-style swadoshi or indigenous self-reliance. It also produces kindness and responsiveness and smiles, so rare so far. Everything in its place, and first comes work. As in China, the first question addressed to someone new is not "Where are you from?" or even "What do you do?" but "Where do you work?" which is amplified to "What organization?" The other thrust is religion. "The phenomenal growth of Sri Avinashilingam Educational Trust Institutions," says their brochure, "is entirely due to the grace of God. . . ." A temple in the middle of the dusty brown campus is filled for twice-daily prayers, 6:15 A.M. and P.M., during which, says Mr. Narayanswamy, "You must pray like a dog, which as you can see is God backwards." There are pictures all over the campus of Ramakrishna Paramahansa, the Bengali saint who was a great influence on the Founder. Other holy men are immortalized with their mottoes inscribed on walls (TO MAKE A GREAT INDIA, THE WHOLE SECRET IS ORGANIZATION, ACCUMULATION OF POWER, AND COORDINATION OF WILLS: Swami Vivekenanda.) This latter personage, further captioned "The Hindoo Monk of India," is depicted in his loincloth in "the shrine," as the temple is called, together with Ramakrishna, Gandhi, Christ, and Ramakrishna's wife, the Holy Mother Sarda ("who lived with him as brother and sister," Dr. K. says. "Like our founder, Gandhiji said, 'The youth should come forward and, remaining unmarried, dedicate their lives to the whole India.' ").

Dinah and Judith smirk at the whole thing, and I can do it too; it's very easy to make fun of these people, but they are getting something done. There is an externally measurable quality to their lives. (Does that count?) If anything has to be glorified, why not, in India, the cult of labor and chastity? What does India need, children or work?

This sort of argument cuts no ice with Dinah and Judith, though. It reassures me in a way to see yet another apparently constitutional difference between us. As in our reading —returned to our room for a rest before dinner, I get back to my nutrition text, Dinah (out of thrillers) reads Teilhard de Chardin, and Judith is buried in Gurdjieff. Any proof that I won't submit to Bhagwan comforts me. I suppose my fear has to do with being a coward in groups, in situations where I flow against the general current. I'm really scared that I won't be able to hold on with hundreds of them pulling at me. In an alien and alienating environment, without the normal tools to measure or the mirrors to reflect, one is awfully vulnerable to the mass. So many, so intense their commitment, so certain of the answer they have found: Will they submerge me? There is a terrible expenditure of energy in remembering who you are in such situations, and it's almost wholly waste. How can I still see and be and watch with all those pressures going on? Coward. Then this line of thought always starts another: If you are a self-diagnosed coward, do you accept it and do the cowardly thing with grace or put up a doomed and unseemly struggle?

At dinner, three or four complicated and exquisite vegetarian dishes served by some of the teachers (who won't sit down with us), we are joined by Ann Walker, a young nutritionist from Reading University who is in Coimbatore to check the figures in the leaf-protein work. (There is a related project at Reading in which she is involved.) She is worried about the publication of statistics, especially optimistic ones, so soon. While initial measurements have shown that the leaf-protein children have exceeded all but the milk ones in growth, "There are many problems and variables," and she feels the statistics so far should not be bruited about lest they be subject to misinterpretation. "It's a two-year project. We should wait." "We" is me, of course, since no one else is interested. I'm reminded of the (white) civil-rights worker I met in Mississippi in 1964 with a similar, if more directly expressed, caveat: "If you write that we have guns, we'll kill you." When it's life or death, keep quiet.

Out of it all, Dinah has discovered a circular pattern in white inscribed in the dust of the dining room threshold and is trying to copy it. One of the teachers explains that it is a koalam, an auspicious design painted on many floors and walls in Tamil Nadu, and there are infinite varieties of them, mostly based on dots with lines either connecting them or intersecting the gaps between. The teacher whips off an extremely intricate one in an instant, and says all little girls learn them from their mothers. From this moment Dinah is lost to us. She is practicing koalams on any surface to be seen, whatever else is going on.

August 3

D r. K. has arranged for us to see the balwadi (nursery school) in one of the experimental villages. Socially, the great innovation has been the introduction of the balwadis in the first place: village mothers have traditionally taken small children along with them to the fields all day, and the idea that at two and a half they could be ready for other care took several months to catch on. The experiment required it, however, as measurements would be meaningless without control over most, if not all, of what the children eat. When parents realized how the children were thriving, there were more applicants than places. Other advantages soon became obvious to the mothers, who often have infants to tote to the fields as well, together with the family's main meal which they've had to cook in advance in the early morning.

We are going to Koundampalayam, the village chosen for no special supplement, just the basal diet (which is meant to be the same for all, and is more or less the normal local menu, but measured and sufficient calorically if not in protein). Mutulaxmi, the teacher assigned to take us, is hesitant, as rain looks probable and there seems to be a general Indian suspicion that their rain is wetter than anyone else's or that Westerners, unfamiliar with monsoons, live in perpetual drought. Persuaded that we know how to use umbrellas, she takes us for a bus ride to the village, which doesn't exactly start but meanders along a dirt track from the main road on. The rural equivalent of the endless cities. The balwadi is next to the school, one room, solid enough. It was built by local labor after the girls of the college volunteered their work, camping there for ten days and digging and carrying to show that everyone could help. Then villagers contributed sand and bricks as well as their own time.

As we enter, there is a shattering explosion. As one, the children sitting in a circle on the floor erupt into tears and screams of panic. Have they never seen non-Indians? "We must seem like escaped zoo animals," Judith says (although for that matter they are unlikely to have seen a zoo). It takes a time for their two teachers to make peace, though snuffles and terrified peeks persist. One question is partly resolved, anyway: the effect on the experiment of the extra attention provided by frequent audiences—these children are clearly unused to spectators, at least our breed.

They are as plump-cheeked as the movie posters, with skin from pale beige to black, clothes of brilliant orange and pink and red, many with kohl around the eyes and very fancy forehead spots with dots and radiations. The girls wear fluorescent bows and flowers in their hair—but then Mutulaxmi tells us that some of the girls are in fact boys, with plaited bowed hair "because the parents don't have a girl." Since obviously in this society there is hardly a premium on the female, this is puzzling. But I remember an Iraqi foreign minister whose parents, after the death of two elder brothers, had his ears pierced to fool the devil (who wouldn't want to bother with a girl), and I wonder whether such a superstition might be operating here. (But the Iraqi was also circumcised according to Jewish not Muslim rites, by a mohel at seven days instead of the Muslim two years, on the grounds that the devil wouldn't want to bother with a Jew.)

The children are recovering, and those not still mute with fear perform for us, reciting and singing, telling stories suggested by a picture, identifying numbers. It all seems like anywhere's nursery school, even the same heart-splitting shrieks from a late arrival as his mother deserts him. But there is a difference: the strange length of time these children can sit quietly. They are obedient, immobile. Maybe it's worth it for the food, or the parents have made them think so—or inertness bred of malnutrition?

At noon, the cook, a tribal woman, appears with an enormous pot and stations herself in a squat on the floor to ladle out its contents. The children are sent outside to dip their right hands in a water bucket. Resuming their patient circle, they are each served a mound of rice with squash, chilies, and dal (lentils). Picking out the goodies first, they roll neat little balls with their clean right hands to pop into their mouths. The simplicity of it: all you need is a tin dish—no furniture, no cutlery. Dinah: "Furniture was obviously the first step in the downfall of the human race. Using intermediaries between yourself and your physical needs—ridiculous what we've done to ourselves." In fact the only object in the room, besides a built-in cupboard of broken plastic toys, is a set of scales for the children's monthly weigh-in.

This is the second meal of the day. They've already had porridge at nine and there's more of something due at three-thirty. It's supposed to add up to twelve hundred calories (previous average intake, seven hundred ninety). Viewing the heaps of food, one wonders how they eat it all. Some even ask for seconds. "At the beginning they couldn't," says Mutulaxmi. "Now their appetites are up so we are afraid they may eat more at home too." Various other factors tend to disrupt the experiment's exactitudes. Dr. K., for instance, on viewing a child in the skim-milk group who was going blind from carotene deficiency, prescribed extra Vitamin A because "a child's eyesight is more important than the project."

I'm not sure what conclusions we can draw from the balwadi, apart from speculations about furniture and the devil. I wanted to go to the leaf-protein village, but it's too far, and the college's only vehicle is in use; but watching sixty other children munching their dark green laddu supplement wouldn't mean much to us without something to compare it to. I do want to taste it though, and when we return to the college Dr. K. arranges for a batch to be cooked up. It's almost black, about the size of a Ping-Pong ball, heavily sweetened and flavored with sesame seeds, and quite delicious after you get the hang of the taste of leaves. They tried many different recipes first, Dr. K. explains (in four years of tests on albino rats and then staff and student volunteers), but the big problem is that there is no good food solvent for the stuff. They tried it as a sort of chutney but it's gritty, won't dissolve. They stuffed eggplants with it, made spicy powders, dal balls in soup, sweet dumplings, and tried to mix it with banana and cereal, until they hit on the laddu, which is a mixture of jaggery (crude brown sugar) with tapioca filler and various flavorings. Sesame is added not just for taste but because it supplements the amino acids.

"Eventually, if it works, what we need is a simpler machine," says Dr. K., "so the village women can do it themselves. Then we'll know it's a real success." There is such a possibility, a machine similar to the oil presses the villagers use anyway; and there are steam generators available for coagulation. "The process is so simple, that's what appealed to us. Anyone can understand it. It can fit right into village life. All the dairying is done by women anyway; the women give it thought."

This is over tea with Dr. K. in the staff eating room where I appall her by smoking a cigarette (there is no ashtray in the college: Indian women do not smoke; and as it is considered polluting to use a dish, ditching the remains requires some dextrous maneuvering). She again laments the absence of Dr. Devadas, but she won't return for some days and we have to leave tonight. Dinah and Judith "want to get to some *interior* traveling."

We have acquired train tickets to Bangalore at very short notice because it is Tuesday. Tuesday is ruled by Mars and full of evil omens for the traveler. Friday might do, though only half as well, as Friday is Laxmi's day and women aren't meant to move: "Keep Laxmi's success in your house, don't let it go." (This intelligence comes from teachers of science.) The ticket seller at the station helps us immediately under a sign THERE IS NO SEPARATE Q FOR LADIES and directs us, as he hands over the precious bits of paper, to "Be happy! You *must* be happy!"

His advice is seconded back at the college where Dr. K. arranges a special audience for us with the Founder. He is a small, imposing old man with sparse white hair and white homespun Gandhian clothes who, after greeting us with the namaste, the palms-together, smiley bow expected in return, says to us only: "Be happy! Happiness is the first condition of growth!" I am partial to this counsel. It is very far from what I have been hearing from my friends.

My body is well again, and the project has left me optimistic. However at our last supper Ann Walker puts what we've seen in a more depressing context. Even starting a proper feeding program at two and a half, she says, is too late to reverse the effects of malnourishment, chief among these "possibly permanent brain damage." Many are born underweight with impaired chances, and from six months when they are customarily weaned, most children never eat adequately and brain cells simply do not develop, nor can they be reclaimed. Although the Koundampalayam children had seemed healthy to me, I recognized in retrospect, hearing her describe them, the symptoms of protein deficiency—the "flag signs." Some have hair that is lighter in patches—"You can see when the diet changes the hair grows in another shade." Others are typically "moon-faced" (I thought they were healthily plump) or show signs of sight damage, with eyes dry and white at the edges. Still others develop kwashiorkor with its characteristic reddish pigmentation of hair and skin, or merasmus, which leaves them thin and emaciated. Many adapt by being very small and stunted, though normally proportioned. "But there is no clear-cut symptom, because a child who is deficient in protein is also deficient in other things. The first call on the food is energy, second is body-building, and what protein they get is all used on energy. Because they've never had enough to eat they can't catch up now; they're very small and they will probably grow up to be small adults." As for those in the experiment, there is a tendency among the children in all the villages to catch up on their depleted resources and then level off. They limit their own calories after a while, stop taking more; but ten grams of extra protein a day can produce measurable results—again, however, we have to wait for them.

Scientific prudence all around. "It is not a good idea," comes the cautionary voice of the Reading nutritionist, "to be too involved in the Pirie camp. He is *obsessed*, you know."

Who wouldn't be? Who isn't? How else do you get anything done? The point is, how single-mindedly, and is it a reasonable obsession? There is Judith, obsessed that the rain will curl her hair. Dinah is grieving because her favorite koalam has been washed away before she got to copy it, though still scribbling others to the end. But both of them are suspended in their Poona-dream, known or unknown; they are arrows in midflight, aiming at that single target. I am obsessed in a completely mixed-up way with everything I see of India, what it means, what to do about it. The Women's College has changed the shape of things slightly. It is easier to connect with the poor as other people instead of as A Problem, but that doesn't make their plight any less a problem.

We wait beneath a bus shelter which we share with two prone figures swathed in lungis, not even a toe sticking out. You can't tell anything about them except that one is a child. But they went to bed early, whoever they are, to make sure of a shelter from this season's unreliable weather. There are some less resourceful people huddled by the station wall. A woman is watching her baby, trying to get him to sleep. He is naked with nothing between him and the pavement nor protection from the rain in the night.

Inside the station we pass a beggar child the size of a one-year-old but with the physique of four or five, with the wizened, shriveled look of an ad for Save the Children. His hair is dull and gray-orange-dusty color and his skin is folded like an elephant's. He has nothing on except a black cord around his waist. This absurdly minute creature is squatting by a wall in a pool of bloody diarrhea. His mother, standing over him, yells impatiently at him and he begins to cry. The mother, an ageless hag who is probably fifteen and as dull of eye and tone as her offspring, yells louder and takes a swipe at him. He shrieks. Would my Freudian friends say he cries because his mother doesn't love him? She finally moves off and in fear he gets up and totters after. Then you see the reason for the bloody mess he's left—a red ulcer the size of a walnut protruding from his behind. The receding view becomes one of those pictures your mind takes that you know will never go away.

August 4

Bangalore. This is the day when even more than usual goes wrong. What are we doing here? Various people along the way have recommended the local caves and temples, but at the station tourist office we learn no buses visit them today, and for us there is no other day. The most popular guru in India, Satya Sai Baba, presides here, but Bhagwan disapproves of him. Baba's darshans draw crowds by the thousands; he selects a lucky few, for whom he materializes, out of nowhere, rings, medallions, and handfuls of dust. The Indian government, through the newspapers, wages a constant and ineffectual campaign against Sai Baba's "magic," showing, among other things, that only the rich receive rings, and the poor dust. Nevertheless many Indians believe in him, and I wish we could visit his ashram, but Dinah's refusal is total.

She knows a local Parsee, the son of her Poona landlord. Perhaps he'll show us around. But a call establishes that he is ill, though we are invited for drinks in the evening. In any case the first item of business once again is to arrange a getaway. Dishearteningly, above the ticket window a complicated chart is deciphered to mean that no second-class places to Bombay are available for *two weeks*, Mars and Laxmi notwithstanding.

We engage a tourist car to take us to the sights, planning to use it first for our errands: to the airline office—perhaps we could *fly* to Bombay. But we fail dismally to convince the manager, who cunningly seats us facing the light, that despite our student cards we are young enough for a youth discount, and the regular fare is more than we've got. Back to the station to book the only alternative, first-class tickets. Traipse about looking for the bedroll man—at least we'll qualify for softness this trip—but he is not to be found. The tourist office guide, whom we have been talked into engaging as well as the car, has his own business: the car needs fuel. This requires a drive to a special office which issues chits, then to the petrol station. An hour's process. The car has an ad in the back window: KUNG-FOBIA. MIND BLOWING MUSIC BY THE FUNKIEST BEAT GROUPS IN THE COUNTRY. A NIGHT WITHOUT END. Meanwhile it's a day without end. Mr. D'Souza in Bombay gave us the name of "my brother's hotel" in this town, but the driver can't locate it because it is not in Bangalore proper but in Bangalore cantonment, and at the hotel, which is found after an exhaustive tour of both, the management have never heard of Mr. D'Souza or his brother. They will accept us however and our dirty laundry, promising to return the clothes in the evening.

The traffic, meanwhile, is as interesting as in all the cities, and the driver as intrepid, his disaster-premonition sense as finely tuned. When you consider that half the secret of driving is an ability to predict what the others are going to do, his feats are truly miraculous, for "the others" are not just motorized maniacs in cars, trucks, buses, and motorcycles but oxcarts, cycle-rickshaws, horse-drawn covered wagons, horses and traps, cows, middle-of-the-road pedestrians, donkey carts, peeing dogs, and the occasional horse meandering up the down lane. The main traffic rules are to remain in the center of the street, pass everything but allow nothing to pass you, and blow your horn (or toot, tinkle, or moo). Above all, never be deterred by the fact that the road is quite impassable ahead.

At last at 2 P.M. (we arrived at 8 A.M.) we are ready for our tour. A Mughal palace, a temple, and the Lal Bagh Botanical Gardens are on the agenda. The palace must have been as dramatic once as the sacking and looting which so diminished it. The temple, like the others we've seen, promises much and delivers little—all ornate elaboration outside and a single phallic image, the famous ghee-smeared lingam, in a dark niche inside, which is in any case shut off by grilles and fences and bars and chicken wire and beggars and touts and guides. Ostensibly the original model for Kew, the Botanical Gardens are unique in that they contain virtually no plants. (These very few are protected however with signs: PLEASE DON'T MEDDLE WITH PLANTS.) The great glass greenhouse is the site of a propaganda display: LET US WAGE WAR ON OUR EATING HABITS. "Eat Less Rice," the public is exhorted, with exemplary pictures of a fat bald man eating rice and a strong hairy man eating salad, banana pie, and boiled potatoes. "Rice/Wheat/Ragi: Fore Go Once a Day" instructs another display. "Use instead Ghee, Cabbages, etc."

Our tour guide is ceaselessly trying to engage our attention with the introduction of each new delight with "I am now going to bore you about . . ." Finding our interest wandering, he mourns "Oh! I am boring you!" But inevitably as we reenter the car it's to the announcement "I have *now* bored you with . . ." and "I will *next* bore you with . . ." Judith takes her leave any chance she can, walking off on her own. "She's avoided my boring," the guide notes disconsolately. We've had enough of each other in all directions; the car was booked for the day, but now when we are blatantly cheated with the news that our time is up, we are only relieved.

Needing respite from this India, we find a posh restaurant, with that anonymous Martian atmosphere prevailing everywhere but Mars, to have an expensive Western meal. Dinah and Judith concur that leaf protein is not for them. "Sweet spinach mixed with iron filings" is Dinah's description. "Don't forget the tea leaves," adds Judith. Having lived together day and night for a week now, we've exhausted quite a lot of conversation and end up discussing death. "Will you at least come back to England when your parents die?" Judith asks Dinah. "Oh definitely! I'm dead keen on death!" No crying at her own demise either, she specifies, absolutely resisting the possibility that she might be missed. Dancing and a lovely pyre, that's the ticket. Will I feel as she does in two weeks?

Back at the hotel, another of those establishments where one is followed and peered at constantly, they have not got our laundry done although everyone is always nodding Acha, Acha, in that semicircular Indian fashion, the head tracing the movements of a smile, which looks either daft or endearing depending on your mood. (When the clothes are produced next morning mine are streaked with orange from having been washed with the freshly dyed things of the others, and weirdly shredded presumably from being beaten against rocks, but very clean and neatly pressed withal.) Somehow we manage to muster enough garments among us to look presentable, if shabby, for our drinks date.

Nothing shabby about our Parsee hosts. They are tall, pale-skinned, and Western, the wife—once a stewardess on Air India—wearing her rings on her fingers not feet, which are in hose and high heels. Two little girls in Tyrolean outfits giggle behind the arras as their little brother the heir, decked out as an English schoolboy, is summoned for our inspection. There is *real* Booth's gin (the distinction pointed out: theirs contains juniper berries while the domestic variety is pure alcohol, though labeled identically) and hot canapés. The house—a model suburban bungalow —is decorated with objects which came from either his or her "ancestral home" and is kept clean, the wife explains, with a terrible effort due to the Indian dust. "Here we have to swab! We get down on our knees!" ("Not hers, I'll ween," whispers Dinah.)

They ask about our families, homes, work. When Judith reveals she is a psychotherapist the reaction is one I'm coming to expect, though writ large. Her job is apparently connected in people's minds to the possession of voodoolike powers. Ever since she started defining herself as a therapist instead of a writer, people go strange: fawning, awe-struck, self-conscious, and full of a respect that is otherwise reserved for Mafia chiefs. Even more interesting is how Judith is changing as a result. She is gradually becoming the image the world has of her profession, inhabiting it with the suggestion that she really does have supernatural forces at her command. At any rate, the news now excites our hostess to spasms of nervous tittering. "I suppose you can see right *through* me!" she says. "You can probably tell all *about* me!" From that moment, conversation is conducted with an eye on Judith, as if her reaction will mirror to our hosts some important piece of information about themselves. Judith assumes a suitably portentous expression.

Another Parsee couple drops in, and they all tell us of their Zoroastrian religion. "We came from Persia because we couldn't stand the persecution." Again this strange time sense: the exodus in question was in the eighth century. "There are only a lakh of us left now." (*Lakh* is the sensible Indian word for a hundred thousand.) Any woman marrying out of the religion is no longer allowed to go to the fire temple, where they worship on New Year's and birthdays. Worse, neither she nor her children can have their remains disposed of in the Parsee fashion—the corpses left on a "Tower of Silence" for the vultures. Although being eaten up doesn't bother any of us visibly, it calls for a seemingly habitual defensive rationale. They speak of how clean, how unpolluting it is to be picked by vultures, why doesn't everybody do it? My speculations on the minimal vulture populations of New York or London, say, provoke insistence that if you leave the bodies there, the vultures will turn up. "It's so *clean*," they keep stressing. "There are four channels for the blood, and the bones are taken away every six months. No *smell*."

On the subject of what, exactly, Zoroastrians believe in while alive, they are less clear. Something about the women wearing their saris the other way around, with the extra flap of cloth on the right instead of the left; and they speak Gujarati and are generally well-educated, rich, and powerful. Yes, but what texts, what ideas? In answer they show us an icon on their bedroom wall, an image of Zoroaster—

though are not forthcoming on what his teachings involved. You get the impression that the religion exists for belonging's sake, a very exclusive club. And that they are in India but not of it. Local political questions don't interest these particular people, at any rate, except as their businesses are affected. On expropriation: "Maybe it's a good thing, but we are against it. Of course."

All four are mystified by mysticism or why anyone should come to India for the gurus. "After all, what is there in life?" asks the guest husband. "To say a little prayer every day, watch your children grow, make a lot of money —why complicate it? Fighting boredom, that is the problem."

August 5

TICKETLESS TRAVELER HEAVY PENALTY AWAITS YOU. LESS LUGGAGE MORE COMFORT MAKE TRAVEL A PLEASURE. This train is a special called the Miraj Express, and first class, so the seats are cushioned. Great bundles of bedding have been deposited at our feet. A coach attached to ours is set aside for "First Class attendants," its slatted benches jammed with women and children as well. Even a constantly moving bench is a better home than the street. We pass forests of tall trees and, in human clearings, stacks of bricks as red as the earth where they're piled in heaps as big as the cottages they're intended to build. Then, jutting up, some bare hills with rocks improbably balanced on top. You can tell we're traveling north: The signs are both in Tamil and Hindi.

We're due in Poona tomorrow morning, but I will stay on the train to Bombay and fetch our luggage. Dinah patiently draws me maps so that I can get back to the ashram afterward. Very late in the afternoon we establish that we are on the wrong train, however. It goes to Bombay, and via Poona, but for some reason we got on a thirty-six-hour inland train instead of the straight twenty-six-hour one which began at the same moment. Too much, the idea of another eight hours to Bombay and back; I'll have to get out with them and collect the bags some other time. Maybe we won't need our clothes anyway, maybe even I will be inspired to instant orange. "I suppose you'll expect me to call you Pankaja when we're there," I grumble to Dinah as the threat draws closer. She just smiles.

I am trying to read a book about hunger. Though saturated with landscape and anything whatever to do with trains, and bored as a Parsee in Bangalore, I simply can't become involved in it beyond a page or two, and then have to reread even that. Dinah and Judith not interested at all. Why is it so hard to care about other people's hunger—not less when its evidence surrounds you? Why after only a week is it so defeatingly dull to be everywhere importuned by petitioners plucking, bleating Ma! Ma! as they do at every station now, dark fingers thrusting through the bars refusing to go away even when crossed with silver (or food), braving any shame and abuse for the sake of their deadly demands? Why is it such a struggle to read about solutions, to connect with it? How is it possible for the few of us who have enough to eat not to become engaged in the *only* problem engaging the *full* attention of most of the world? Just guilt? But it's *not* my fault. Is hunger like pain-memory—unreal when you're full? Anyway what can I do? Giving to one beggar or a dozen solves nothing, sparing a thought to the problem achieves even less. The impotence of pity, the pity of impotence. (What about the impotence of impotence, the *pity* of pity?) We pass another exhortatory billboard: HELP THE POOR SAVE THE NATION. What does it mean? Help the poor *and* save the nation or help the poor *to* save the nation?

August 6

This is the Miraj Express all right, Mirage Express more like it. We've stopped at Gubbi and Banasandra and Arsikere and Birur Jct. (Change for Shimoga and Talaguppa Branch) and at Miraj at 6 A.M. they rudely wake us, grab away the bedding, and make everybody change trains. Now we're going through Rahimat-pur, Adarki, Kirloskar Vadi, Phursungi. Outside in flashes: a woman scrubbing two water buffalo submerged (all three) to the neck in a stream; AVOID RUMORS AND LOOSE TALK. DO YOUR DUTY; a multicolored step temple hidden in a tiny valley; two boys sitting on a wall playing flutes; a goatherd hooded in a split burlap sack in a sudden rain torrent; BOGUS RATION CARD HOLDER IS NEIGHBOR'S WORST ENEMY; the calls of the vendors on the station platforms as we stop. One step up from beggary—try to sell you figs or guavas, biscuits or sweetmeats, dumplings or pancakes, each sung in a different tune, a contrapuntal street song: Victorian London must have sounded like this. Pools from the monsoon rains make little mirrors in the deep green fields. It occurs to me that while the monsoon is proceeding on schedule and as billed, I have not got wet. On the other hand I have had enough of these trains. As the journey's odd chronometer, a Muslim marks the hours off with prayers in the corridor, very loud but without self-consciousness. I have found a place to sit where I can try to concentrate on hunger, but two businessmen start a conversation. They make whiskey and gin, they say. Any samples? "We don't drink." Why don't you put juniper berries in your gin? I ask. What are juniper berries? they ask. "Would you care to visit our plastics factory in Bombay?" says one. Before I can work out a polite form of No thanks, the other businessman starts to berate his friend in their own language (Kutchi) and then they explain, very embarrassed, that since the "Humairgency," foreign visitors like me require government permission and applications to their embassy; there is also at least a fifteen-day wait. Thinking I can at last get some talk about this Emergency, and the alleged collapse of democracy under Mrs. Gandhi, I follow up with a harmless question about how else it has affected them. But evidently they no longer understand my English.

Poona!
Dinah takes charge, organizing us into two motor rickshaws (so designed that the side openings are too low for vision but perfectly suited for falling out if you don't cling with both hands, not easy with bags to hold as well—the

whole contraption being springless, jolting perilously over the road's ruts and crevices) to 35 Koregaon Park. Rented when her children came, her house was kept on as a home convenient for sannyasins, as it abuts the ashram. The park, a British leftover, is full of rich estates, improbable art deco next to turreted Victorian. The overall effect is of a posh subtropical suburbia—old trees, palm and frangipani, houses set back from the road and neatly gardened, privileged privateness. I think of San Angel, the outskirts of Madrid, Havana's Miramar.

Dinah's warnings about plumbing have prepared me for something distinctly makeshift: but the rickshaws pull up at a villa fit for a rajah, now overgrown with jungle. We've passed increasing numbers of orange figures drifting around the roads and there are many more within the gates of 35. Pillows, mats, and bedding on the deep veranda, mosquito nets marking off the boundary for this little domestic settlement or that, hint at the amazing number of sannyasins resident here. In and out they troop. "Who's that?" I ask Dinah. "I don't know," she shrugs. "But isn't it your house?" She is in agony at the idea that it is indeed her house and, just when she's most anxious to rejoin her master, she is bedeviled with domestic trivia. People just show up and sleep here, she laments. Nobody pays the slightest notice of *her*. For that matter nobody pays.

Still, she has enough influence to empty some space when she needs it. Judith and I are allocated a tall airy room between the main common space and Dinah and Stuart's porch room. (Today Stuart is scheduled to emerge from his speechless "Primal," so presumably he will consent to a roommate, though a note left for Dinah suggests an absence of welcome and announces he'll be out the rest of the day.) There is one high, narrow bed in here draped with netting. "Someone's pinched the other bed," moans Dinah—it seems an ex-resident of our room became antibed at some point during her absence in London and threw it in the garden, where it stood in the rain until rescued by a porch-boarder who, being pregnant, has intimidated Dinah from asking for its return. Judith volunteers to sleep on a mattress but Dinah's not even sure what became of all her mattresses—or sheets, mosquito nets, lamps. Through Clara, the maid, something is located (though "the Danes say it's theirs"), and we sling up nets for it from the overhead fan and are off to the ashram to sign on for darshan.

Instead of a walk around the block we take a shortcut through a building site—the ashram is swallowing as many of the neighboring estates as it can afford to buy, and lately, due to a freeze on real-estate exchange, is extending its constructions within the gates. Odd villas of indeterminate age and style, but mainly white stucco, are juxtaposed with giant pits where foundations for others are being built. Everywhere the orange creatures waft, their loose robes lifting in the breeze, a glazed and inward-looking aspect to their eyes which makes you think of one-way mirrors. To the sound of distant drums we gingerly cross a mammoth pile of dirt on which dark, scrawny women and children crawl, loading it by the basketful to their heads; the children stop to beg from us. None of them are wearing mirrored dresses.

"What about the mirrored dresses?" I ask Dinah.

"What are you talking about?" she says.

A path precariously skirts a ditch the size of an Olympic pool and just as wet, but full of floating turds. A sign announces that, presumably given enough basketfuls of dirt, the ditch eventually will become the "Vipassana Meditation Hall" (named after the ashram ghost, the sannyasin whose death and incineration last spring had so moved Dinah). Teetering over builders' boards beside the hovels where the workers live and the villas of sannyasins, past an even larger, oval building site, we arrive at the back end of the ashram, entering next to Bhagwan's house. Overgrown and fenced in, it is invisible. In a clearing surrounded with elephant ear plants, four sannyasins are tenderly bathing a white Mercedes.

"What's that for?" I want to know. "I thought you said he never went out."

"Laxmi uses it, I think." Laxmi, she explains, is a high-caste Bombay lady who has been with Bhagwan for ten years and administers the place.

Activity everywhere—a makeshift canteen is selling tea and meals beside an open-walled room where a noisy meditation is proceeding (the drums explained) and all around are standing, chewing, lolling, strolling orange people. In my violently blue dress—blue has never seemed a violence before it was surrounded by so much orange—I am feeling very odd. There aren't many Indians around, and they stick out too—mainly because they look quite natural in their robes while the Westerners are somehow gelatinous: the very long floating locks and gowns make everyone from behind or a distance look like an amoebic blob. Nearer to, about a quarter of them have beards; and a few women have shaven heads or the crewcut which attests to a recent confrontation with their hair. Only the very young and clear-skinned look attractive. I suppose artifice is frowned upon, impractical, or smells.

Around the corner we can see the gardens, thick with flowers, an occasional sannyasin weeding or contemplatively washing the paving stones, mala stashed under one arm. Pictures of Bhagwan hang not just around every neck but in every gap of wall. Change the face to Christ or Mao and we could be in church or China. Why is it so necessary to see him everywhere? The true mark of a society without choice is the ubiquitous eye of the leader upon you. Is there no security without? *The need to feel watched*: now there's a question.

In the office building, which confronts a ghastly modern fountain and the main entrance, an even more hideous arched gate, sannyasins sit at desks on a porch receiving others or dealing with ashram business. A typist, head in earphones, is transcribing from a tape recorder. Passersby drop in to sift through stacks of mail with more than the difficulties one would expect in a place full of transients, because not only are people on the move but so is what they're called. Silly old Western friends and mothers can't (I gather from the talk) acquire the knack of spelling out correctly their new Ma's or Swami's names.

Any effort to join in conversation or exchange a friendly smile is rebuffed. The danger of a stranger, and *blue*. Have to wait it out. I find a notice board with displays enticing one to various groups, in different handwritings, some illuminated with tantric doodles:

> *Vipassana Intensive*: A 10-day experiment in witnessing—without interruption or distraction of any kind. a. Sitting. b. Walking. c. General mindfulness.
> *Movement Group*: gentle bio-energetics, fantasy. Mime and dance.
> *Structural Integration* (Rolfing).
> *T'ai Chi Ch'uan*: for me it's a way of awareness, and slowing down, getting centered, getting high. Open Group or Intensive (full).
> *Zazen*: Nothing special. [This one illustrated only by a mirror.]
> *Primal*: Bhagwan has said that this course is to create a situation where people can let go thru their fears and madness, their obsessions and secret desires in a safe,

protected environment, where help can be offered to see beyond. In Primal the door is FEELING: subjectivity as experienced thru the child within.

Massage: "Massage is needed in the world because love has disappeared . . ." Bhagwan Shree Rajneesh.

Soma: [Illustration: Rorschach violets, "Now" penned in the middle] . . . means "Moon." Bhagwan Shree Rajneesh means "Lord of the Full Moon." Soma is a 15-day non-cathartic group. Implosive. We develop our intuitive faculties in areas such as psychic massage, telepathy, dream-state awareness and astral projection.

Nadam: Music meditation.

Hypnotherapy: A workshop in letting go.

Tathata: Tathata means suchness. It means no fixed structure, just let whatever happens happen and flow with it. 24 hours continuously from 9 pm to 9 pm. . . . Bring a towel and that's all.

Dinah says there weren't any groups when she first came in 1974, but that when people from the "Human Potential Movement" turned up, Bhagwan suggested they try their specialties at the ashram. Now half of each month is devoted to these activities (the other half to meditations). Bhagwan assigns sannyasins to the therapies he thinks will help them, or they choose themselves. Many of the group leaders support themselves here by this work, though all profit goes to the ashram and the leaders get nothing but board and lodging. The Primal costs sixty pounds, says Dinah. "You have to pay or you wouldn't get so much out of it." That's nearly a thousand rupees. The ragged workers in their abysmal shacks are paid two and a half rupees a day. What are they getting out of it?

We are summoned finally. When she hears we've just arrived, Arup, the darshan-appointments maker, signs us

on for Sunday, day after tomorrow. The English "camp"—
when Bhagwan gives his daily lectures in English rather
than the current month's Hindi, and when the program of
meditations fills the day—starts Wednesday.

"Do all these sannyasins live in the ashram?" I ask Dinah
on the way home—for we seem to have passed hundreds of
them. Only three hundred or four hundred actually are in
town, she guesses, during the Hindi camp, though more will
come next week. And only a lucky few—certainly less than
a hundred—have rooms at the ashram itself. "The others
have to find digs in Poon," she says. "Some of the places are
pretty rough, but it depends what you can afford."

"How do you earn money?"

"You don't, really. No one's paid for ashram work, and
that's where everyone wants to be."

"So what do people without incomes do?"

"They have to get it off someone who has."

She talked about the kinds of work that Bhagwan assigns. Quite often it's a kind of trick. He wants you to do
what you *can't* do, or deliberately gives you the most un-
suitable job to "shake you up." An English friend is editing
the darshan books, for example, just because she felt inadequate with words. Others are assigned to clean the lavatories, and if they hate it they are told to do it until they
love it.

"What's the point of that?"

"It has to do with the feelings about yourself that the
work provokes. If it really brings you down to clean a lavatory, you have to get into that and come to terms with it. If
you can clean the lavatory and not get connected with it,
then you're free of it." At the moment, she says, there is a
young upper-caste Indian minding the loos, since the work
is particularly unspeakable to him.

"But who's ever going to love cleaning lavatories?" I am

much perplexed. "How could you, unless you shut off part of yourself? And isn't that the opposite of what he's trying to do?"

She gives me her patient, you'll-understand-someday look.

Clara has cooked dinner by the time we get back to 35, and various pots of rice, vegetables, and custard share the table with brown vials containing evil-looking pills and fluids. Their owners, I am told, are suffering from random aches and pains (brought on in the struggle for self-discovery) which these tonics, prescribed by an Ayurvedic pharmacist, are supposed to eradicate. This pharmacist is such a genius, says Dinah, that he cures "hep" (atitis) in *three days*; and is so proud of his—secret—remedy that he refuses payment, instead soliciting contributions for a local home for retired animals. (Retired animals?) The hep convalescent to whom she refers—an English-speaking German like the rest of them—is opposite me, chewing after the fashion of a ruminant ("He's getting into eating"), gazing at his plate upon which he has mixed all his dinner ingredients into a sort of mush, the sweet pudding together with the lentils and rice and vegetables, never once looking up to verify this tale of which he is so remarkable a hero. It's the end of dinner-table conversation, such as it is, though a German remark surfaces from time to time in the reflective silence; but no one mentions our arrival among them or asks who we are, and their own sannyasin names, only revealed after the second or third direct request, fail to hook into my mind as they all sound the same and seem to start with *P*. As a sort of *aide-mémoire*, I ask one woman what her name used to be and she stares at me with silent horror as if I'd asked her what her daddy did in the war.

After dinner, Dinah sportingly suggests a drink at the

Blue Diamond, the best hotel in Poona, which happens to be around the corner, and where sannyasins go to enjoy the air conditioning, telephone, change money, buy stamps, or use a lavatory cleaned by someone else. Posh and snooty—to the limited extent that a modern hotel can manage, i.e., rude—it must have been designed to cash in on some short-lived tourist boom but is home now largely to Arabs and the distressed mothers of rich sannyasins. Several gin-and-lemons later I decide that this is just the role for me: distressed mother. After all, my main concern is why Dinah should turn in motherhood, and for what. She is not offended when I speak of it; but then she is still being solicitous overtime. All those Poona buildups including descriptions of the blissful Blue Diamond, where you can get cool and pissed right down the street, are now made manifest as we are edged gradually into the rigors, whatever they are, of real life at the ashram.

August 7

Now I see what went wrong with my clothes in Bangalore: the Indian laundering technique is demonstrated by Clara as I sit in the line for the bathroom. She beats them to death, whacking each wet garment full strength from high above her head onto the rough rocky side of the well. The ringing thwacks give a tempo to the sounds of early morning: a garbled song in no-man's-language coming from the bathroom, tropical birdcalls, the whistle of passing trains, and Stuart's cough, which is actually more of a death rattle. I haven't seen him yet, but Dinah, who joins me in line, reports "He looks a fright! He's lost a stone and he only weighed two to begin with." As the cough approaches it becomes a species of sob, and Stuart (oh, all right—since he looks so pained when I call him that—Devopama), almost invisibly thin and translucent, lowers his bones to sit with us. It wasn't too primal after all, his Primal, I gather: They weren't so much delving into a deeper past as attacking current relationships. He spent a lot of time doing to a mattress, which represented Dinah, what Clara is doing to the clothes. Dinah looks pained. What else? "Lots of exercises," he gasps, "like a half-hour hoo with our arms linked together—awfully difficult that way—to get the energy flowing." He is interrupted by a desperate spasm of coughing. "Then you'd freak out on your mattress for an hour and a half." The problem was the mattresses were wet, in fact the whole room was flooded from some heavy rain last week, but they couldn't move because "it's a specially soundproofed place for freakouts." Having spent a fortnight there, Stuart, Devopama, seems unlikely to survive the next. He breathes like an advanced emphysemiac. "What did you eat," I asked, "to get so thin?" "Oh, simple food, just yogurt and dal. *Delicious* when you're so hungry." As for his health, he must get down to the Ayurvedic pharmacist straight away. He has a very solemn and as yet inconclusive attitude about the entire event, and I see I am neither to laugh nor feel sorry for him. He's getting into himself. Everybody's getting into something.

Getting into the bathroom is another matter, but eventually a scraggy blond person nobody's seen before emerges, and the three of us go in together. No time for modesty around here; we take turns on the lavatory and splash cold brown water that's stored in the bath (in lieu of any coming from the taps) over ourselves with plastic jugs. Dinah is fretting seriously now about what to do with all her unwanted, unidentified boarders, rehearsing admonitory speeches soundlessly. Clara, wringing her hands and sari, had come to her lamenting their numbers and the impossibility of regular food budgets when people sneak into the kitchen and steal, leaving such a mess that the rats eat the rest. Indeed I got the impression last night that there wouldn't be much breakfast. When we came back from the hotel we admitted a tall, brown-bearded fellow who immediately made for the kitchen where, humming, he spread butter on a platter full of bread and, still humming, ate it. Dinah wasn't up to dealing with him then, and most of the stealthy moochers who sleep on the porch tend to dematerialize in the daylight. At breakfast (Clara came with new supplies, expecting the worst), only the official Germans remain. When not conversing in their tongue they are as impenetrable in their silences and it's clear they won't, as hoped, supply clues about themselves or what they're doing here. Oh well, it leaves you lots of space to get into your food—which consists, among such concessions to the Western palate as boiled eggs and porridge, bread and butter, of mounds of amazing fruit I've never seen before with names like chikku and custard apple. You can also study the décor. Behind the corner German is an altar with Bhagwan's picture and various little stone and shell offerings. Bhagwan's picture is all over the house. (Later, a German who is doing translations for the ashram starts work by first propping her Bhagwan picture up before her to scan as she works.) Otherwise, the tall room contains some rudimentary living-room furniture, a padlocked wardrobe and a sofa, toads, lizards, a crazed, screaming kitten half the size of the rats it's supposed to catch, and some very beautiful landscape photographs taken by the landlord.

Whom we are now to visit—to bring news of his family in Bangalore and to try to mollify in case he's noticed all the camp followers who have turned his sedate villa into an international slum. Mr. Rastomjee has a jewelry and clock business on the way to the town center. A small man with a constant, lit-up, toothy smile, he mourns the passing of the raj, and immediately attaches himself to us as if we were its last relics, gracious with coffee and shows of his prize-winning photographs and offers to take us sightseeing. Having lived in Poona for seventy years he has seen it become a major industrial center, but the happy memories are of the war when the English were stationed here in numbers and you could get decent talk and music. He used to play the violin in an English officers' chamber group. At one point he invented a gadget to turn the pages of sheet music and "even Yehudi Menuhin took it up! He said I could give his name to it!" but nothing developed, and his beautiful wife died, his son's business moved that family to Bangalore, his daughter married outside the Parsees, and business isn't up to much these days. Who can afford jewelry or clocks?

When he shows us around a temple it is with great civic pride, yet Mr. Rastomjee has clearly not visited it since the last Britisher left, and is disconcerted at having to remove his sandals (revealing socks, the only socks in India), unfamiliar with the protocol. Still, feeling safe with him as front man—because he is a man at all, however un-Hindi, in this misogynist atmosphere—we circle around the puja ceremony, an offering of fruit and flowers to the gods, as the Aums and incense fill every space. In the dim light with the odd smells and strange gesticulations before their offerings, the priests and worshipers seem at least about to raise the dead; but when they're gone, only a few limp flowers remain.

We toil endless steps and ramps up Parbati Hill to a temple above the edge of Poona; the view almost makes the climb worthwhile. Here it was, says Dinah, that Felix was felled with sunstroke last year. She was always trying to liven up the children's time with little expeditions, but in his case everything went wrong. Like Dinah's mother, who came out to get the twins, Felix refused to so much as lay eyes on Bhagwan, as if in fear of some fatal communicable disease. Emily went and even took sannyas, but when the great one gave her a name he said meant "Immeasurable" she took him to say "Miserable" and was quite put out, even though she got a cake that night to celebrate her new birthday.

Down the hill again Dinah, still breaking us in gently via the evasive temptations of extra-ashram activities, bundles us along to Mahatma Gandhi Road ("the Bond Street of Poona") to look for cloth so that we can have robes made. It's a very Western town. Many people have given up their comfortable saris and lungis for skirts and trousers, and the shops are signposted in English and sell a strange array of specialized goods suggesting affluence. There is a tropical fish shop. The "Choice Centre" advertises NYLON SOCKS BELTS TOILETS LOCKS. The fabric emporium is furnished with lengths of mattress on which to sit (shoes parked at door) while bolts of cloth are removed from the shelves and unrolled in luxuriant swaths at our feet. As at an auction, the merest nod gets results, usually the wrong ones, and more and more bolts are unwound on our laps until we are buried and further than ever from a choice. All I know is that I won't have orange.

We meet Devopama (who looks better already) clutching a stock of disgusting brown substances from the Ayurvedic man and repair to a sweetmeat shop to eat bowls of rus malai and taste one of everything else. Trays appear of pink, green, yellow, and silver, celestial substances with no relation to the products of Messrs. Hershey and Cadbury, which seem by contrast about as appetizing as the contents of Devopama's bottles.

Returning to Koregaon Park and its concentrations of rumpled orange figures, I suddenly realize what makes everyone look so weird. Although it is late afternoon, they all seem to have just got out of bed. Dinah greets in passing a tall, distinctively smooth personage whom she explains is Teertha, an Englishman who lives in Bhagwan's house and is Very Important. He looks it: a kind of angelic Rasputin.

I have sent a telegram to my father's friend Mulk Raj Anand, who has a weekend place nearby, and after dinner he turns up at the house. I've been counting on Mulk, a novelist whose books sell in millions and equally active as magazine editor, traveler, and professional radical, to be my socialist-realist anchor. But the instant he arrives he shows not the wary doubts I anticipated, but the most exuberant congratulatory glee at finding me exploring what is to his mind "the only solution for Western youth!" I cannot believe it. This man is an old red, Soviet-style. "Everyone ought to come!" he bellows. "I'm looking forward to the day when this ashram takes over all of Poona and Poona is known just as the place of this ashram! Because I want all the world's youth to come. The more that come, the less there will be left to fight wars."

I'm able to insert a question about his admiration for a setup in which a fellow takes over as God: How can one maintain an independent search when one man's word is law?

"A father figure is needed," he replies, "like a professor

at university. Deepening the personality is a gradual process. To find depth and tenderness and gentleness is hard and long, and a guru is at least a transitional necessity."

I am adrift. My last potential support has given way, and now I'll have to face this business on my own, without another point of reference. At the same time it's easy to see that nothing better could have happened—and Mulk thinks I ought to stay for months, invest myself entirely in Eastern spiritual discovery here and all over the place. Suddenly, lit up with his enthusiasm, the view of the next two weeks—all I've got—seems pathetically inadequate. I go to bed mumbling phrases to address to Bhagwan tomorrow night while Judith and Dinah wash their hair.

August 8

Wash hair, wash hair. It so happens I have washed my hair every day of my life for more than twenty years, so what's another shampoo? I am famous for my shampoos. I wash my hair even if I have to walk miles for a jug of water or have just had a baby or 103 degrees. I refuse to get excited about such a minor matter. But I have washed it, presented my head perfunctorily for Dinah's approval, and she says it stinks. I have washed it in scentless soap twice, but the smell of twenty years of old shampoo lingers; three washes later it still does. Judith too.

When we are not washing we are drying, lying among the thick garden weeds to catch the sun, getting ready for the next wash, and smelling each other. I can't smell a thing: What is all this? "Don't worry," patronizes Devopama, "it's quite usual to freak out. Everybody does." At least half a dozen people are turned away from darshan every night, it seems, for failing the sniff-at-the-gate test—which has become more stringent lately because one woman slipped through with a perceptible odor of perfume and it made Bhagwan sick the whole next day. Some people have been turned away six or eight times. And rejection has a way of happening just when you need acceptance most. Devopama has a friend who, having just broken up with his wife, needs Bhagwan's counsel desperately but has been sent away twice now. He writes the Master letters and receives the reply, "When you come to darshan we will discuss it," and writes back, "But I can't get *in*."

Wash hair, wash hair. "Make it a meditation" is the irritating advice as I am sniffed and failed again. "Get into it." My brains are numb from being dunked into buckets of cold water for half-hour stretches. I warm them in the sun again, trying to read to forget how ridiculous I feel, and aided by the distraction of two of the house's residents (French, friendly, but they do their own cooking so are not present at Clara's meals). They are taking snapshots of each other around me, which wouldn't be especially notable except that one of them is eight and a half months pregnant and naked. "You smell fine," they approve my hair ("We are into affirmation"), but Dinah flunks me yet again, together with the verdict that *hot* water is needed and in vast quantities, or I'll simply never pass. The only answer is a shower at the ashram. Why didn't you say so to begin with? Draped with scarves and towels "to prevent picking up dust smells," we traipse through the building sites, pay the upper-caste Indian lavatory attendant a rupee each, and submit to the shower for half an hour, until the entire hot water supply is used up.

I have washed my hair eight times. I am the butt of a very odd jest, and convinced by now that the whole thing has been organized to catch me in my own fetish—washing your hair *every* day is one thing, washing it *all* day is another. But also it resembles a trick devised by Grotowski or Gurdjieff (they've got me reading Gurdjieff) to raise the stakes of one's participation so that the investment in it overwhelms the possibility of toying with the encounter lightly. No danger of that by now.

Admittance, passing through the gates, comes almost as a benediction. We have been gathering at the entrance, all of us with darshan appointments, early and anxious and scrubbed. Most have been there before, but all must listen as Shiva—a red-bearded Scottish sannyasin who seems to be chief bodyguard—intones the drill before the smelling starts. He grimly recites and amplifies on the rules, more or less repeating the inimitable ashram language as displayed in the office:

> 1. The time for Darshan is 6:30 P.M., at the gate of Lao Tzu House.
> 2. Take a bath without using any perfumed soap or shampoo—a hot water or cold water bath is enough [*sic*].
> 3. Cleanly washed clothes, full length are beautiful to wear.
> 4. For keeping the feet clean, chappals or sandals are good.
> 5. If the body is suffering from sickness or infection then let it recover first and make a new appointment when the body is well again.

6. For sannyas, when your name is called, just get up and sit in front of HIM at a little distance with closed eyes. When the mala is given just be available so that He can give the mala easily and the name.

7. If you have anything to ask or say, you can do so, or just sit in your place.

8. Asking or talking can happen when your turn comes.

9. If Bhagwan Shree suggests that you come back to see Him on a certain date, please come to the office the next day to confirm the appointment.

10. Those who receive sannyas or who receive a center's name are requested to go to the reception desk immediately after Darshan and fill up the form for the ashram records.

11. Any letters, photos, etc. that you feel to give to Bhagwan Shree to see, can be given at the office between 3:30 and 5:30 P.M.

Personal questions about Bhagwan are not permitted, Shiva adds. And if anyone "feels to cough," leave the Presence until it's over. Two coughs and you're out. Do not go nearer to Bhagwan Shree than a meter. Do not touch him except his feet. If you are turned away, wash harder next time. With that, he and his accomplice Maneesha, both obviously born clean, start turning people away. As the names are read out, each aspirant runs the gauntlet of their joint noses poked into the hair, looks exchanged over heads, then a "no" or an "all right" which sounds almost grudging. We who have passed look at one another with unnatural relief. I am quickly past the thought "Maybe I could have got away with seven?" and wondering what in the world to say to this demanding god.

Abandoning the rejects, who cling with staggered disbelief to the other side of the gate, we troop through the foliage down the side of Bhagwan's house to the outdoor auditorium where, Dinah says, he also speaks each morning. There are perhaps twenty of us but not all will actively participate: Dinah's here just to accompany us, for instance, and among the others is a Tao group—he sees all groups before they disband. We sit in rows on the smooth stone floor under a roof half open to the trees and sky and before a dais where an ugly modern armchair waits. It is twilight and the mosquitoes are homing in, having spread the word that here there is no insecticide. Maneesha fiddles with a cassette recorder; we sit in abashed, expectant silence.

A door opens and out come three women. Dinah tells me later who they are: Laxmi, the ashram administrator, a pale Indian lady who they say ceased to eat some years ago; Vivek, who is Bhagwan's English "shakti" (the word for the female divinity linked to each Hindu god—or his woman, in other words, though what that amounts to is a matter for speculation, since he has transcended sex); and Mukta, a Greek heiress who, with Laxmi, footed the bill for the ashram's beginnings. Vivek is holding a handful of malas and a transparent plastic clipboard full of paper, with which she stations herself on the floor by the left arm of the chair. The others join Maneesha on its right.

And here he is in his sleek white robes (synthetic: allergies), smiling and nodding a namaste (palms together) in greeting, a towel over his arm in the manner of a waiter, except his towel is monogrammed YSL. I've seen a thousand photographs of him, but none of them suggests how astonishing he is. The eyes are alert and calm at once, radiating a kind of final authority made quizzical by unusually arched black eyebrows. There is a brilliance to them, a smooth sheen to his skin, and an overall grace which makes you lose a breath and stare. Despite his middle age, he reminds me of a child who is not beautiful but more than beautiful because of its childness, a time before the skin becomes an old coat and is still a tight, translucent part of the body it wraps. You are aware of the perfection through one life of all life. He seems so healthy: I have never seen anyone look healthier. Why all the anxiety about the imminent failure of this body? Another trick? If he's really rotten to the core they've done a remarkable polishing job. That's it: He looks polished, buffed, like very expensive fingernails.

The first name has been called; someone is taking sannyas. He has greeted her and she crouches on the floor before him, eyes shut, while he contemplates her. Finally he writes with elaborate flourishes on the clipboard, removes the sheet of paper, exchanges the clipboard with Vivek for a mala and says "all right." The new sannyasin opens her eyes and bends forward to receive the mala, which he puts around her neck and continues to hold with one hand as the other covers her head. He has the tapered, mobile, expressive hands of many Indians, though a distinctly Brahman pallor. I can't hear anything he's saying and am preoccupied with mosquitoes, wondering how many times you're allowed to scratch before they turn you out. Bhagwan himself hasn't this problem as Mukta and Maneesha tenderly brush aside any tiny predator aimed his way. It is almost dark and the trains are whistling. Most attention-stealing is that pest Shiva, the bodyguard and hair-sniffer, circling around like a bat in the night taking hundreds of flash photographs. A media man, our guru here. Even if I can't hear him six feet away—the dialogue is sotto voce in deference to the personal nature of some of the matters discussed —it is all being taped and will be published shortly by the ashram in an illustrated book.

141

Very gradually some phrases stick out from the jumbled mumbling and I hear him explain to the initiate what the new name means. While it is difficult to change your personality, he tells her, and thereby rid yourself of all associated miseries, it is another matter just to *drop* it. You will find that your old problems and anxieties were "all there in the name" and the identity it represented, and while you could "paint it, decorate it, modify it . . . basically it remains the same." This old identity was called "Barbara," and now "Barbara is dead, gone forever and she cannot be retrieved." Instead he proceeds to call her something meaning "Divine Remembrance," with a small lecture on its significance. Everything is divine, he says. Nothing in creation is or possibly can be wrong or can disturb you, as long as you remember that it too is divine. The devil and his insults, anything. She is advised, should she find herself losing it, to remember this feeling, because what we remember, we grow to become. After a small exchange about her occupation (schoolteacher) he continues to the effect that there is never enough of God and indeed of bliss, of peace, of love: the more you drink, the more you thirst. The whole concept of *enough*, in fact, is a problem of insecurity which comes from the greed of the mind. People want even more than is necessary in order to feel safe. But with God this is impossible: "One starts the journey but one never ends it." Divine Remembrance is incandescent as she floats back to her place.

An American summoned as "Caroline" is in no time "Kalayani," which means "blessing," and she is encouraged never to take life for granted because it is a gift of God and the fact that she has been granted it is an affirmation of God's acceptance and love for her. "The whole wills you to be, the whole celebrates your being, the whole is happy that you are." He talks to her about the way people give their lives for money, honor, religion, politics—but that you cannot sacrifice your life for anything because life itself is the supreme value, nothing is higher.

Three Indians follow and receive short shrift, the mechanics of sannyas and out. He barely glances at them when selecting names, dismisses them, and they don't seem to care: having started in a swoon and bent low to kiss his toes, by the time they have their malas they are somewhere I have never traveled.

Next it's the turn of two men who are leaving the ashram to go home. They are each presented with a mysterious little box and encouraged to feel that Bhagwan will always be with them.

Judith is called. She looks stricken and smitten at once, but almost instantly relaxes as he asks her questions and she tells him that she has been traveling around in the south before coming. He doesn't expressly disapprove—you get the feeling he doesn't do that—but warns that travelers are habitually traveling, and she must make the effort to stop moving, if only in her head, and really be here.

Because the sin of traveling is mine, not hers, it seems a pity Judith has to own to it, and I hope she isn't daunted. But he sweeps on to the matter of groups, and assigns her to two—one of her choice and one of his, which she may not enjoy, as people tend to resist that which will most affect them: "they cling even to misery if it is familiar."

Now he is talking to the right person. Will Judith have to reconsider her attachment to misery? Maybe something will come of this.

I hear her say, in answer to some question about work, that she is "an analytical psychotherapist." She is familiar enough with his ideas to know he has expressed a fair amount of derision for her colleagues, and was anxious about this moment. How brave to jump right in! She talks of a parallel interest in encounter groups, and his response is unexpected. Rather than take sides and make judgments, he suggests that the two forms of therapy, since they work in different dimensions, can only enhance one another, and that her experience in both is most useful. One covers a lot of ground, one goes deep, and both are necessary. While analytical psychology is out of date in its neglect of the whole person, he says, encounter too can be criticized for its superficiality, and what really is needed is a synthesis of the two—like a child of mixed parentage who is "something new, more alive, because those two parents are so different and their meeting has great tension and challenge in it." At this point he even pays his respects to Freud—upon whom he usually pours wrath and scorn—as an innovator who brought different systems together; and advises Judith to reconcile the contradictions between the two movements and use her unique position to cross-fertilize. Out of them may come something "bigger, higher, deeper than both."

In some invisible way it is clear that he is finished and Judith returns to her place as I am called.

"What about you?" he says. His eyes don't blink and seem hollow. The idea of being nervous seems ridiculous, because I don't feel separate from him, and he's not nervous. His *attention*: He is there with me, in and around me, I'm surrounded with awareness. Not a small share of it is my own: for what, after all, has been my objective, in the weeks since the idea arose, but this moment? At any rate the words come out, and after hearing myself say "I don't know why I'm here since I came through the generosity of my friends, not in the usual way," I am astonished to hear me telling him that I am happy, as if I've just discovered it about somebody else, and even more amazed to realize that it is true. "I have found three things in my life which give me joy, divine joy. My work, and being in love, and my children. I want to try to see if there is more, because I am unable to understand what has drawn, what has magnetized, my friend Pankaja" (the official text published later then reads: "Bhagwan chuckles") "to give up her children to be here."

"You will have glimpses" is all he gives me in answer to my question about Dinah. The rest is to me. "Children and work are good, beautiful, but not the end of the story, just the very beginning, the beginning of the beginning. Much more is waiting. And for people like you, much is possible very easily. People ordinarily become interested in meditation only when they are miserable, only when they have failed in their love, only when they have not been able to be joyful with their children, only when their work is frustrating them. So people come to meditation in a very negative mood. Even then, meditation gives them deep glimpses of joy.

"So for a person like you . . . it is very rare to find a person like you who can say, 'I am feeling joy—not just joy but divine joy—with my children, my work, and with my love.' It is very rare . . . these people have disappeared from the world."

Throughout this singular speech, and particularly now, I feel like yelling False Pretenses! The fool's believing me! and making weird faces. If I make the faces, Shiva fails to record them in his photos (he is flitting about behind Bhagwan clicking and flashing—Befores and Afters?).

Bhagwan continues: "So for people like you, meditation can become a tremendous transformation because you come with a very positive background. That's why you don't know why you are here. People who come out of misery know why they are here. They have some problem so they have come to solve it. You don't know because you don't have any problem."

This is a bit much. *"I have problems!"* I break in, but he continues, "No, in this way—you are not miserable, you are happy, you enjoy your children, your work, your love; you have something in your life which you cherish, you feel a sort of contentment with your life. Everybody has problems, but those problems have not destroyed your work, have not destroyed your relationship. So those problems are growth problems—everybody has to face them: They are good, they enhance life. But if you start with this background, a sort of happy background, positive, then much more is possible because you will be floating with the current —and people are fighting against the current. Even then, they attain to many blissful states. So just try."

He asks me how long I'm staying and says to put my mind aside and meditate. "Meditation will enhance everything. It is not against anything, so whatsoever you do, it will make you more contented. You will be a *better* mother, a *better* lover, and your work will be ecstatic." This is what I heard him say. In the official text the list is different: "a better wife, a better lover, a better mother." Who was talking about wives? Who wants to be a better wife? (Who for that matter wants to put the mind aside? Who wants to do the dynamic meditation?)

"People who are too interested in the result, miss it. But I can see that it will be possible for you. Come back to see me on the fifteenth, mmm? Goot."

The fifteenth is in five days. By then will I have some proper misery to offer him? I almost wish I was in crisis, to see what he would do about it. But it's not possible. My head feels as clean within as it indisputably is without. Another visitor is sitting with him now, an Italian woman in obvious anguish to whom he is saying, "You are carrying the whole Catholic Church around you." She is directed, too, to return on the fifteenth. Then two or three sannyasins with personal problems to discuss. To one he says "Surrender to life, then you can be happy almost twenty-four hours —day in, day out, year in, year out." If happiness comes from his "surrender," and I am already happy, what does it say about surrender? I think as we file out. "What was in the boxes that he gave those men who are leaving?" I ask Dinah. "Hair from his beard and a toenail," she whispers.

Dinah is dancing. "Now I can do my own trip," she skips about with glee. Now she can stop worrying about us all the time. She has handed us over, delivered us safely.

At dinner I am in a daze and don't hear them until they ask me about the darshan. I talk about my true-or-false pretenses, and who am I to be happy? Whereupon Judith, in a picky mood, snaps: "But that's your line—you always put over this idea that you're okay and don't need anything."

"Well I am okay." (For years I have had to defend myself against their constant therapies, these two, but eventually you can forget what the words mean. How are you? *Fine.*) "I mean, I'm *okay.* But *that* okay? So that it becomes my definition? That's not just presumptuous, that's absurd. I suppose I haven't thought about it enough. Don't you just take it for granted that you're as miserable as everybody else? Maybe it's not true?"

Their confusion may well balance mine, but how can they discuss it? After all, Bhagwan now has stamped his official imprimatur on this happiness of mine. I think I am in some sort of corner, but not sure in what room.

Anyway Judith has rounded on Stuart and the subject of his sannyas. He got the name Devopama and his mala by mail (having sent a photo from London) and Judith, describing her impression of the ceremony, thinks it's really too bad he didn't wait to do it here. He's missed all the poetry; why doesn't he do it again? Dinah rebukes Judith for being horrid to Stuart. Judith says she wasn't either being horrid to Stuart. They argue schoolgirlishly and at length and sulk off to bed.

August 9

At 4 A.M. I am brilliantly awake and clawing aside the mosquito net to get up for dynamic meditation. Tiptoeing to the kitchen in the dark to put the kettle on, I encounter only rats and a lakh of cockroaches but return to find Judith in the same alert state, so we call it a night. I have never felt more awake. "You have nowhere to go but *up*," I hum to myself, having abstracted the basic message of the night before. The idea that I shall feel any better than I do already is too heady to contemplate at dawn, especially a perfect one.

It is too dark to try to negotiate the slippery paths by the building sites so we walk the proper way around, by road. Beneath a bridge is a mass of huddled shapes still sleeping. Judith says she saw a bear there yesterday. A bear? "Of course," she affirms. "Why not? Some sort of performing bear, I suppose. Perhaps it helps them with their begging." I try to discern something pawed and furry among the heaps of limbs in rags, but her vision is not vouchsafed me.

Other bodies, the ones we find assembled in the meditation hall, gain instant definition when the Indian sun rises, abruptly as a light switched on. It's the same old frenzied-treadmill music as in London, but there are improvements. The smells can escape through the open back wall and the silent mime-scream catharsis helps me to concentrate on my own pain excavations. Perhaps it's not without value after all, I am wondering on the way home to breakfast, though the thought collapses at the sight of the workers' hovels by the hole they're digging. Two small boys are crouched in the entrance of a hut made of Esso tins and straw, one washing his skinny arms in a pail, the other combing his kwashiorkor-red hair in a broken piece of mirror. A tiny girl with a swollen belly scratches patterns in the dust with a stick. And I—strong in the sun, headed for a good meal—have just had to be *inventive* to conjure up some agony appropriate for catharsis. There is no way coherently to assemble, let alone resolve, these images, made even black-and-whiter by the vision of a little girl no bigger than the one playing in the dust but blond, dressed in orange and a mini-mala, in the lap of a male sannyasin gate guard who is showing her the pictures in a *Time* magazine. It can only be seen as two distinct worlds, theirs to starve and serve us in the pursuit of our incomparably sophisticated—compared to their organic—pain. How much longer can we afford ours? What do they see when they look at us? When they are grown, who will those two small girls be to each other? —the dark one by now irreversibly damaged by malnourishment, the light one already introduced to the priorities of *Time.* In this way, by allowing brown babies only scraps of life, pink people can maintain *Time*-style priorities for at least another generation. Nutritional imperialism.

Bhagwan's discourses switch to English in two days' time, so in order not to miss any of them I've got to go to Bombay tomorrow for our bags. At the station I am able to present myself, unruffled through custom, at the awful number of counters required to book a place on the Deccan

Queen (an ultra first-class conveyance for the Bombay rich who weekend in Poona). Decide to walk around town and, passing a bank, to change some traveler's checks. From the line at the counter marked Foreign Exchange, where two clerks send customers to an officer at a desk to have their signatures witnessed, I am returned to the clerks for more witnessing before being directed to "Eleven number counter" and presented with a brass disk. At Eleven number counter, nothing is happening except a woman reading a Hindi novel. This is obviously going to be one of those Indian all-day paperwork spectaculars. People I've seen at the ashram drift in, non-orange—a bad sign, we have obviously not chosen the way of the initiates to transact our finances. But during the wait we make friends.

One of the women is my successor at darshan last night, the one "carrying the whole Catholic Church around her," but she has obviously discarded it already. She is a clothes designer from Milan named Fiorenza, and she looks better this morning: almost unrecognizably jolly in fact. The trouble about yesterday, she says, was that she'd just finished a Rolfing session and was in several kinds of acute agony. The point of Rolfing is to release muscle tensions which mask emotional ones, she explains, and in her case manipulations of a specific spot in her chest had let out ancient, hidden memories physically filed away there and suddenly present and to be accounted for. But she doesn't know which torture was worse, the violent pummeling from the Rolfer or the resulting psychic bruises (for some reason no somatic ones).

Fiorenza and Karen, a young American with her, both have just arrived independently in Poona after a long guru-quest throughout the subcontinent. Like me they are rather cynical about the idea of orangery as a route to nirvana, though unlike me they think there *is* a route. Fiorenza's discoveries about herself and her possibilities began with a

Milanese encounter group, "the best experience of my life," in which, in a single weekend, she "learned to touch and feel again." Her work—providing fashion designs for cheap labor to execute—brings her to Delhi annually and after it's completed she takes up her pilgrimage where it left off the year before. Karen, a quiet, intelligent girl who'd been on the drug/hippie circuit from Kashmir to Rishikesh with her husband, had heard of Bhagwan from a sannyasin encountered along the way. The atmosphere of the place intrigues her—"It's like a summer camp. You're warm and fed and someone tells you what to do all day!"—but she hasn't had darshan yet because she's sick, so hasn't laid eyes on the Master; and now her husband is not only "really getting into it" but is incommunicado in an "Enlightenment Intensive," and she is feeling, to say the least, left out.

Eventually, very eventually, our money comes through and we walk back toward the ashram through the crowds. All the men are wearing Day-Glo plastic bracelets—it's some festival in which sisters give their brothers bracelets in exchange for presents—and pavement booths sell more bracelets. Passing a mob urging on a fight between a cobra and a mongoose while a boy in a trance lies in the middle of them with cataracts of blood, or something rather like it, spilling from his mouth, we exchange horror stories of India and I am getting to feel like an old hand, which is salutary and lamentable at once. If you can be callused enough, India need not interfere with the soul's search. But what can a soul perceive through calluses? That is worth the cost of them? I suspect it is as Ruth Prawer Jhabvala put it: "Having once seen the sights in India, and the way it has been ordained that people must live out their lives, nowhere in the world can ever be all that good to be in again."

Back home, Dinah is getting moody, a brood hen, refusing to speak beyond informing me that she was up all night.

One of the German girls has a notice pinned to her robe reading SILENCE, which doesn't make much difference in her case, and Dinah wants to do the same—an old ashram custom apparently—but is still beset with landlady responsibilities. There are the accounts to sort out: Clara says the week's shopping money is already used up. It's easy to see why at lunch, when she presents us with a large expensive fruitcake for dessert—after a big meal all of us together can eat less than a quarter of it, and it ought to last a day or two. But when I pass the table half an hour later there is nothing but a sliver left. Who ate it? Other people, guests of guests, unlicensed lodgers, one big fruitcake bandit? Or those who, having eaten, discovered a latterlunch void? Dinah, in reaction, is getting fierce with scavengers and starting to speak her rehearsed mouthings aloud. She has got the bed away from the pregnant German, demanded that intruders account for themselves, insisted that a room intended for a Dane cannot accommodate four Danes on one Dane's rent, and tried to wrest from the reluctant what they owe to Mr. Rastomjee. But what she really wants to do is work on her book, a memoir of her Bhagwan experience which he has assigned her to finish. *Her own trip.* After sitting with a distracted stare over the meal, she's off immediately to sit in her room, plaiting her hair as she writes and smoking beedies, the local spicy smelling herbal cigarettes, each tied round with a red string bow. For lack of an ashtray or a desire to get up and fetch one, she simply stubs them out on the chair's wooden arm, transcribing her dictations from heaven. It wouldn't matter if the moon burst or the floor floated off; when Dinah works she is oblivious and as always she fills the yellow pages with her small, unedited scrawl until forced to stop in midsentence, picking it up again later without apparent difficulty. By the day's end her hair is poking out in funny bits of braid and the arm of the chair is neatly heaped with butts and ash.

Judith, too, is chewing over some private matters. She answers questions in hard-edged grunts and initiates no talk herself. There is an impermeable casing around her stretching for tens of yards and requiring one to keep (at least) that distance. Thus we traipse over to the ashram in sight of one another and yet not together for the kundalini meditation, tremble violently for twenty minutes, dance for twenty, rest for twenty more, then back home, still separate. I am feeling so good: I wish I could tell somebody.

Getting ready for bed, I remark to Judith that this experience must be as traumatic in its way as being in China was for me many years ago, since, now as then, my period has stopped. I'm chattering away about "Women don't menstruate in war, you know," wondering how this qualifies, when from the next room the voice of Devopama observes, "Maybe you're pregnant."

Don't be ridiculous. It's not possible. Out of the question. Is he right?

August 10

In my reclining seat in the Deccan Queen, which is to other Indian trains as a Rolls to an oxcart, I am obliterated. Thinking I may be pregnant, all things change. I know now what I didn't yesterday: that compared to this,

I *was* as happy as Bhagwan—if not I—observed. But that my three divine conditions are just that: conditions. I can survive on the operation of just one of them, as I usually have to, though I must have at least that one to survive at all. But they're operative only within a general equilibrium. In another state—the fourth?—everything might fit and I might not be so demolished by a single, speculative blow: my holiday blighted, the freedom to see and think beyond this anxiety gone, a familiar torment having taken up residence in my belly as if it had never left. Yesterday with no decent excuse for catharsis I had to summon up the almost forgotten image of my husband and his girlfriend in order to contrive something to weep over. Indeed, I could weep, and hit them and hit them, but resentment was remote compared to last year, even last month. *Feeling* was remote, in fact—the thing they're all after. And yet since Devopama's remark, as if I need some *extra* reason for misery, I have been wringing myself out over the ludicrous detail of guilt over smoking, aware that smoking lowers birth weight —again even now I am smoking, right now, this minute torturing myself as I simultaneously entertain the thought (knowing it cannot be anything but an entertainment) of actually having the child. What child? I'm not pregnant.

And what is to Be Here Now in this, pray? I am on one of the surely most exciting and beautiful train journeys in the world, wonderfully alone for the first time in weeks, with a perfect breakfast of omelet, buttered toast, tea, and a banana delivered to my seat, *India* rushing past, en route to a day in Bombay, a lunch date with Mulk Raj Anand and the prospect of new friends, and it's a strain even to observe the monkeys.

(The monkeys. Everyone in India is a supplicant, some more successful than others. The train pauses beside a tremendous gorge with a two-thousand-foot waterfall cutting through the mountains. A party of monkeys scampers up the incline to beg and is inundated with bits of bread and banana from the windows. Starving children at the stations are ignored.)

I seem to *need* blindness like this—through some devised pain if not my anesthetics. Now instead of experiencing what is there or even thinking of Bhagwan and the importance of what is happening, I take refuge in this triple stream of confusion: wondering first how to plot a secret abortion here in India, wondering second how to go through with it, and recognizing fundamentally a wondrous repose in the idea that it cannot possibly be true in the first place. I am quite, quite mad.

TRY. Bhagwan says don't try: *be.* That's the general motto, anyway. To me, he certainly said Try. And it's only effort that will distract me, God knows. Who?

The Deccan Queen. LET US GET ON WITH THE JOB OF NATION BUILDING it says at the end of the coach. The train contains a very anomalous group: fat Indians. To find a trainful at all I would think you'd have to ransack the country, and here they all are, talking English to each other, wearing suits, peeing in a Western lavatory. (A letter of Abu Abraham's in the *Illustrated Weekly of India* I bought at the station says: "I have always believed that this country can politically be divided into two classes: those who sit on Western-style commodes and those who squat Indian style.") It is pouring outside, all space so thick with rain there is no room for air, just as it always pours when I'm under shelter, and a second-sighted waiter refills my cup the instant it's empty. The train really is a Rolls, with graceful chrome fittings designed precisely to hold a tray, a cigarette, a glass, an *Illustrated Weekly.* Businessmen are making deals, gross children waddle by in pursuit of amusement not alms, and just to prove that this monsoon will never wet me, the rain abruptly halts as we approach Bombay and I see a woman tottering through a rice paddy with a folded umbrella balanced neatly on her head.

First stop is the tall block of flats where live the parents of an Anglo-Indian friend who has sent them a letter with me. By the elevator is a sign: SERVANTS AND HEAVY LUGGAGE NOT PERMITTED. I wonder how the servants decide which luggage is heavy enough for them to carry to the top. Welcome flows in the form of Jamaican rum and, from my friend's mother, a cacophonous argument about the ashram. While at first it feels comforting to find an ally in spiritual skepticism, I soon feel oddly displaced and, in confronting the wall of her dogmatism, hear myself defending aspects of the Bhagwan cause. You don't have to reject *every*thing, I'm saying; you can't call them all misled fools; we can all learn something from it. Blanket dismissal. "Why don't you just come along with me to the club," she suggests genially. She is famous for playing golf every afternoon of the year at the club, no matter how hot or wet. As for the rain, which looks about to resume, "I'm not a rainconscious person. As a matter of fact I'm not an anythingconscious person." I wonder if she is conscious at least of the possible implications of this remark, but she looks only proud.

The clouds, because I'm outside, have blown away. Walking to Mulk's in the kind of sun reserved for me and the mad dogs, who aren't around, I'm full of rum and doubt. The world is divided into people who think they are right, said Lincoln Steffens. Why is one forced into the position of jury with a choice of two verdicts? I've just had to play God's little advocate when as far as I'm concerned it's not a matter of guilt or innocence, all or nothing, yes or no; these dichotomies leave out the middle space for maybe, why not, let's try that. On the other hand I didn't have much room for maybes a month ago. Where is it all going?

Mulk says, "What we have to give you in the West is love. And we have it. But it's disorganized. That's the thing about Rajneesh: he's organized." Mulk won't call him Bhagwan though, and doesn't see what caused him to abandon his previous title of Acharya (teacher). Also, while he would like to visit the ashram on one of his weekends in Poona, it's a bit much to expect him—a venerable figure both of age and repute—to squat at another man's feet. To reasonable doubt of this kind it is impossible to explain that the devotees of Bhagwan's divinity are unlikely to make exceptions; and Mulk's plan, to have a heart-to-heart with the Master without so much as a single shampoo, has little hope of realization.

Whatever his age, Mulk has more energy than any seen Indian (not counting the unseen Dr. Devadas). From his house full of ethnic traveling-trophies and books enough to stock a university library—where he has spent the morning writing on another of his own while his wife held a dancing class in the living room—he is off to his afternoon occupation of magazine editor. I accompany him to his office where masses of people come and go on urgent business (or perhaps to sample his office's unique air conditioning, which puts him relatively in the Bhagwan class), and the simple witnessing of all this activity wears me out. It's time to fetch the bags and return to Poona.

Pass a street stand selling stuffed cobras. My children would love one of those. Negotiations. "How much?" "Thirty rupees." "Fifteen." "Hah!" I walk off. He chases: "Last price?" "Fifteen." "Okay, twenty-nine." "Hah!" I walk off. He pursues: "Very last price?" "Twenty." "Okay." Everybody happy. A taxi driver is watching this performance: "Do you want a taxi, mem sahib?" When I'm in it: "Do you want a real cobra, mem sahib?" He tells me how to catch them, digging them out of their burrows with a forked stick tail-end first. I decline.

It's a very long drive out to the airport hotel and he has a lot to say. A Christian ("My grandfather made that mistake"), he was educated by missionaries to believe in a go-getting scheme of things which has no outlet. "We hate India," he says, not defining the We. "We hate the Indian people. They cheat. They dirty." Leaning on his horn, he points to a skeletal man lurching through the traffic, one of many: "Look at this donkey. Even when they have no work, nothing to do, they want to die quick."

I am also looking at an evil-smelling cart beside us full of chunks of alien animal, which the driver says is shark; and at a crew of sign painters laboriously filling in the colors on a huge billboard on which the letters are already stenciled: DISESL OIL; and trying to see the driver himself in his mirror: very young, slender, average brown, with beautiful wet black eyes. Oh, the trials of taxi driving in India! The owner of the car takes 90 percent of what's on the meter and the driver is lucky to clear twenty to twenty-five rupees for a fifteen-hour day after paying for petrol and crooked policemen. "They just have nothing to do so they pull me to the side and then we have to settle the price. Ten rupees, usually. Then they let me go. But if I meet two in one day I have nothing for my family." As it is, most of his income goes for school bills for his three sons ("Small family is good family," he recites one of the ubiquitous government slogans); the cost of school uniforms is the current crisis. But they must be educated in order to leave "this terrible place." The school teaches them English which he supplements by taking them on Sunday, after church, to an English or American film: "They like the guns and fast cars."

By the time we've arrived at Dadar it is twilight and people are starting to light fires, do their toilet, and bed down on the pavements. The driver has picked my brains about all conceivable spots he could move to, but it's clearly hopeless. There is no way to explain that his racism against his own kind is insignificant next to that elsewhere, and what visionary immigration officer would look past his brown skin to the Calvinist the missionaries planted inside? His grandfather had indeed made that mistake. He leaves me at the Poona taxi rank and I leave him the outrageous tip his tale deserves before settling in for an even longer ride, four hours over the mountains.

Before taking off, the new driver, obviously the traditional breed, does a series of sacramental genuflections like a one-man speeded-up masonic demonstration: knocking his head, touching his left this with his right that, mumbling incantations with accompanying twitches. This is a religious business: the windshield is almost obliterated with effigies and beads and flowers, and new prayers are intoned to get us around each bend—the choice moment, it would seem, to overtake whatever is ahead. It's all accomplished with one hand anyway (the other for his nose) and during the frequent showers it's also done through only half a window, i.e., that half he can reach around to wipe from the side (no wipers). For lack of a seatbelt I am trying to find a purchase on anything besides the floor, but the handles have come off the door and the three men in the back are all gripping the back of my seat tightly, so it's just as well about the prayers. Soon we pass the edges of Bombay, half-finished constructions whose armatures are already overgrown with moss and black mold from the monsoon. Pointy mountains loom into the mist, Himalayan, with mirages of impossible lamaseries on their summits. The trees are straight from Dr. Seuss, skinny poles with tufted pompoms sprouting out the tops. As it darkens, the driver has a trick with the headlights, only turning them on when actually converging on the competition, as if their use were otherwise improvident. I'm beginning to gain confidence in him, actually. He is pelting along passing absolutely everything before him but it's soon clear there is one thing that makes him slow down: a bump in the road. He is taking care of his springs. And he knows that road like the shrine that is the inside of his car, for he anticipates the terrain well in advance, careening over to the oncoming lane to avoid a rut here, a gulch there, even in the dark. If he's made this trip often enough for this degree of familiarity it's reasonable to assume he can make it once more.

Still, it's a relief to stop at a roadhouse, the Sangam Beer and Bar Rest. "Sangam," I have read, means "literary academy." The wall menu reads "tomatoo omlet, non-veg and allpunjabi dishes availablhere." The rickety shack is completely covered with lizards, and in the steaming darkness cows wander about among the garbage, small boys try to sell me something in boxes but can't communicate what, and the best illumination comes from the Coca-Cola sign. The driver and the three other passengers come back chewing betel leaves and the rest of the trip involves much spitting of gobs of mucoid red juice out the windows, rather a feat for the fellow crammed into the middle of the back seat. I am feeling as if I fell out of a Waugh novel.

We make the four-hour trip in just over three, which is not unexpected, and in a style which has quite taken the edge off my troubles. The main thing after all is survival. Do it as it comes, and life is God, and here we are.

August 11

Judith and Dinah aren't speaking to each other. Neither are they speaking to me to tell me why, beyond Judith's contribution: "It is finished." This at 5:30 A.M. as she's poking in the suitcase I brought for something to wear. Dinah has removed every scrap of an orange garment that she'd previously flung liberally around for Judith to borrow.

Today the "camp" starts: a full schedule of meditations as well as the talk in English. The program is stuck up at the main entrance's "Gateless Gate"—a lavish construction, which could not be more gateful, of marble and brass-studded wood. Poking out the top is the ungraceful ashram insignia, a dot in a triangle in a nonagon uncentered in a circle—all of it like a weird upward-gazing eyeball.

    0600–0700 Dynamic Meditation
    0800–0930 Discourse by Bhagwan Shree
    1000–1100 Natraj Meditation
    1400–1530 Taped Discourse
    1600–1700 Nadbrahm
    1730–1830 Kundalini Meditation
    1900–2000 Gaurishankar Meditation

To participate in all this, everyone buys a one-hundred-rupee book of tickets for the ten-day "camp."

We are sniffed as we enter for the discourse, though not so scrupulously as for darshan, and having just washed my hair with shampoo I am ordered to sit at the back. A huge pile of sandals and flip-flops and bags builds up near the gate, as in some tropical death camp. In the auditorium a reverent silence in the crowd waiting. As more people enter (three hundred? five hundred? eight hundred?—impossible to estimate because they're not in proper rows), we're urged forward on the silky stone floor which is already painful, particularly on the ankles as Dinah warned. Bony Devopama has successfully smuggled in his blindfold for a bit of cushion but anything seen to be a potential softness is confiscated. Only a long robe that you can bunch up beneath yourself makes the posture bearable.

Is heaven orange? Seen together, Bhagwan's followers—or all in Poona at the moment—are less a show of types than of type. The few non-sannyasins stick out like strange weeds in an orderly field of corn. There are Fiorenza and Karen and a few other new arrivals in jeans; the distressed mothers, three or four of them, strikingly American in their tourist polyester; and the odd local Indian. The rest are wearing their commitment in a solid mass of orange, though subtly varied from peach to burgundy, even a Sikh in a tangerine turban. Most are under or around thirty, with hair much longer than is still the fashion, androgynous in their flowing cloth. Many eyes are shut and the hush is meditative, total. Only the birds carry on their songs, flying in through the open walls from the young trees beyond to roost on the rafters a while; and Shiva, the orange-haired photographer/bodyguard, casts noisy glances about the floor to seek out potential malefaction. Nothing disruptive can occur except from the back, anyway: like Laing's, Bhagwan's most reliable stalwarts block the front rows.

The door behind the dais opens silently and the three women slide in, then Bhagwan, nodding with his palms-together greeting to a similar response from the crowd. He is dressed the same as at darshan, long white robe, a shirt beneath with gold cufflinks showing, a towel over his arm, black sandals. Microphones beside his chair lead to a tape deck and to a public-address system. He sits.

The first voice to be heard is that of Bhagwan's chief lieutenant Teertha, English, disembodied, reading the parable around which Bhagwan will build his speech. This month the theme is Zen. "Bhagwan. Butai, emperor of Reo, sent for Fudaishi to explain the Diamond Sutra. On the appointed day, Fudaishi came to the palace, mounted the platform, rapped on the table before him, then descended and, still not speaking, left. Butai sat motionless for some minutes, whereupon Shiko, who had seen all that had happened, went up to him and said 'May I be so bold, sir, as to ask whether you understood?' The emperor shook his head sadly. 'What a pity,' said Shiko, 'Fudaishi has never been more eloquent.'"

For the next hour and a half, Bhagwan talks around this story. The combination of rhetoric, comedy, analysis, allusion and exhortation, insult and gentle force he employs is his own and not really describable. His voice is his perfected instrument. He can stroke and lash with it, joke, denounce, and almost sing. In all the speeches I have read and heard on tape or live, there has not been a repetition of so much as a phrase except deliberately within the same talk. Although the same kinds of things are being said over and over, he always says them in a new way; and apart from the jokes brought in on paper, there are no notes, but neither is there an unpremeditated pause or a moment's doubt. He talks thus every day of the year, his hands making delicate gestures like birds, and the hypnotic quality of his message is such that it ceases to be *his*: While he could not be more entirely there, he is not there at all. I think of a poet I knew who heard voices dictating her verse. She only had to write it down. It is Bhagwan who speaks, but he seems more a vehicle than a source. And like other great speakers I have heard, I felt he was addressing only me. The power of this quality was hopelessly diluted, I see now, in my reading of those transcripts or even listening to a tape. At one remove you can appreciate the content and admire the skill of its presentation but you can't be so captured that, as with Fidel, if he were to point at me and instruct me to die on the spot my heart would stop. And yet quite a few of the people around me are apparently asleep. As Dinah told me in London he doesn't mind, even encourages it, on the grounds that the guard of self-consciousness inhibits the penetration of the words.

The words. He is talking about thinking, and the need to stop. There are some concepts here which I find hard to put together, not least the riddle of dealing in concepts at all when the aim is to ditch them; but his intensity and conviction make me willing to suspend my disbelief. Thinking, he says, is always involved with the past and the future. In the present, there is no thought: the present is just experienced openly and as it is. Reflection on it is already no longer in the present. But even this truth, or any truth, cannot be perceived by the mind: It is felt by your entirety, by your "heart." Those who insist on carrying the mind with them are crippled by its weight of memories and projections, and are unable therefore to live the present fully.

He tells the story of Lazarus, dead and buried until Jesus, who loved him very much, came to the grave and told the mourners to stop weeping and wailing because he would call Lazarus back to life. The dead man's sisters scoffed: "He is now stinking!" But Jesus, when the stone was removed, called into the tomb: "Lazarus! Come out!" and indeed Lazarus came out.

Now, he would like us to understand, this is our story. We are moribund, stinking, and he would like to scream at us: "Lazarus! Come out!" We are trapped in our minds, unable simply to *be*, to sense the eternal truth, in desperate need of rebirth out of the ego. We are unable to see what joy, what beauty, what mystery surrounds us; stuck in old concepts of religion which are dead, which are mere *theology* (obviously a dirty word around here), which have left behind the celebration of life, the dancing and loving and song of existence. But you do not need a theology, a faith: you need only your eyes, your awareness of the wonders around you.

Bhagwan is getting a lot of help from the birds at this point. He talks at length about Fudaishi and expands on all the characters in the story. The Diamond Sutra, he says, contains the highest of Buddha's sayings: and what they amount to is the sense that life is far too vast for explanations, that the infinite universe cannot be contained in finite ideas. "Unless you can find someone who has become awakened, you can't sort it out. You can go on repeating it, you can even enjoy the music of your repetition, but you will never be able to penetrate into the mystery.

"Let me tell you Lazarus is *your* name!" He is in a fury with us now: We are in a stupor, we are missing life, and it is our very complacency about understanding that prevents us from understanding. He is shouting to us daily, rapping on our heads, never mind a table, yet we keep on missing it. It is not that he is telling us the truth, because the truth cannot be told: he is trying to wake us so that we can see it ourselves.

"Drop the mind. Stop thinking. Become more alert. See the trees and listen to the birds with no screens of thought. *Meet* directly. Truth is immediate, radiant, here, now. It is not that truth has to be discovered, only that you have to become aware. Truth is already here. Let me shake you, allow me to shake you out of your sleep. Don't go on thinking you understand. Your knowledge is a way of ignoring the truth. Knowledge is the barrier into knowing. When knowledge is dropped, knowing flowers. Enough for today."

With that he rises, flings the towel over his left shoulder, and exits. His audience is indeed in a stupor. No one is prepared for the ending, and nobody moves. When gradually some get up to leave, others approach the platform where he just sat, though the chair has been instantly whipped inside by Shiva and helpers. Prostrating themselves, half a dozen sannyasins touch Bhagwan's floor. In the audience other supplicants stretch full length in the direction of his ghost. Still others meet each other with smiles, tears, embraces.

"Enough for today" is apt indeed. It's only nine-thirty and I have had enough for today. But there are some new meditations to try, first natraj, which turns out to be forty minutes of dancing to a taped, indifferent flute, then twenty minutes of rest. The meditation hall is full. This is a popular one. But the music doesn't move me, and I feel clear and strong enough to dance to birds instead.

After lunch, during which I am a sort of clearinghouse for the others who aren't speaking to each other, Dinah and I return to the ashram for the taped discourse. People unroll mats and settle down for siestas, taking Bhagwan's sleep injunction to rather an extreme, but you can't hear the voice very well for the echoes anyway. It's a nice snooze, enhanced by the idea that, in his opinion, he's got through to me as well. Not to the conscious mind, however.

Three more meditations to go. The nadbrahm is familiar from London, though no less peculiar. To the sound of bells, on and off a normal Western scale, we hum. When the whole room is humming together to a kind of harmony, "It sounds like they are lifting you to heaven," observes Fiorenza afterward. Other times the notes don't match and the dissonance is dreadful. I am aware that such considerations aren't meant to enter into it; but what is? What exactly is the point of all this? "He's working with energy" is Judith's opinion: "Westerners need to work through an excess of energy. We're not ready for the quiet kind of meditation yet." Dinah says it's to "fill the time with nothing" to get us away from the idea of productive activity. "I don't think there is anything wrong with productive activity," I meekly protest. But—no thinking. Actually I am thinking constantly, mainly about a question for Bhagwan with regard to today's talk. Every other day his discourse consists of answers to questions chosen from those submitted the previous evening. Humming away, then going through the next phase as the music changes—hands slowly out, hands slowly back—I come up with it through its very contradictions, and later put it in the box: "I have been thinking all day of a way to ask the question: How to stop thinking?"

Fiorenza materializes beside me on a bench where I'm waiting for the next meditation. I suddenly realize that she is *orange*. And she will take sannyas, she says, at our darshan on Sunday. What happened? "I've learned that in this place it's not wise to ask these questions," she says, "because they have no answers." We sit in silence. I light a cigarette. Two children nearby are hurling sticks and snarling. "Are they trying to blind us?" says Fiorenza. A burly Indian is shouting, I assume at the children until I hear his words "No smoking! You go outside!" Very rough with me. I didn't know. The children continue to hurl sticks.

Beyond the Gateless Gate sannyasins loiter, buying tea from a little cart and smoking, mostly beedies. Fiorenza and I find a wall to sit on. Feeling distinctly threatened, I resume the attempt to understand her. This time she finds an answer, even though there isn't one. She was talking to someone earlier, she says, and decided in the course of it that she was excessively critical of everything, the result of too much ego. She has always suffered from too much ego, she decided, and it is time now to drop it. For instance with a lover, if she has a fight, she doesn't feel like making love afterward. (This seems perfectly reasonable to me, but when I say so she comments that one has to live more in the now, not the past.) Anyway, she had to take the leap, she says, and went straight out to buy an orange lungi and some trousers, felt silly for a while in them, but now is quite content, *right*.

The sudden distance between us shakes me. An ally gone. Have I got too much ego, to even look at it this way? At the same time in general I think I haven't enough, and never had. Always felt no-account, if only as the perpetual outsider.

And overwhelmingly excluded. Outside even the official outsiders—as sannyasins seem to feel about themselves. I think of Polly in London, about to come here after radical and gay politics failed her—continuing her need for identification with a group which is whole, itself, intact, identifiable, but *outcast*. I also feel outcast but find the whole condition contradicted by becoming one of a group of outcasts. This is negative ego, my identity. I cling to it, I need it like my spine: to be unlike everyone, a foreigner everywhere, English in America, American in England: there is *no* one who is *any*thing like *me*. To don a uniform, to find support and comfort in an alliance with others—what true exile could endure it? Fiorenza says she had had "this feeling of unwillingness to submit to others," and that she has conquered it. I can't. I don't even understand why anyone should want to. Without doubt I'm a foreigner *here*.

Later on I bump into Karen. She is still not well enough for darshan, and her summer-camp enthusiasm has diminished markedly. "These people are shit!" she remarks, as though originally. "They're really contemptible for a community of religious seekers. But 'community,' hah! It's a misnomer anyway—like what common cause have they got except what serves their own ends? They say they get off on him, but all they're getting off on is themselves. Honestly, it's pitiful!" But she can't continue this outburst—she must run to see her husband (and exchange notes, since he still isn't allowed to talk). At least she gives new life to my doubts.

The kundalini meditation is almost enough to make me stop thinking. The first phase requires vibrating to snake-charmer music interspersed with what sounds like shrieking train whistles. Once I've got the knack, the trembling wipes out everything. Thought, anyway; but not awareness. I am aware, for instance, of a small Indian boy opening a cupboard in the wall beside me to reveal a woman sleeping, a ragged bundle. Part of the building crew. He shakes her awake and she leaves, rewrapping her sari. More meditation. Minutes later another woman appears, picks her way through the sightless tremblers, and enters the cupboard, shutting the door behind her. Perhaps whole families live in this cupboard, sleeping in shifts. What on earth do they make of this extraordinary bunch out here?

Seeing them with her eyes, I cannot recognize the race at all. Who are these shaking, entranced dreamers, orange or half-naked, eyes in orange masks or clamped closed, locks flying and scattering sweat, limbs flailing the air—a massive epileptics' convention, a massively unattractive mob of dervishes, well-fed brats with checks from Daddy? Speaking of Daddy, there is Bhagwan's old chair on the stage. We are invited to use it for inspiration (a chair?) but not to touch. Perhaps these people need a Daddy—the men so generally frail, both of physique and spirit, the women so strong, as if they all had come from matriarchies. Dinah has always said she needed a father and found one here.

Stop this invading mind—it hasn't even the justification of its origins, the women in the cupboard. The sound is changing anyway, signaling the start of the next phase, dancing. I want to dance. Andean-type flute and concertina music, like an art-film soundtrack. Eyes shut, I revel in my sweaty body as it rolls to the music. I can do it too, even if there are distractions to shut out, the sounds of hammering, sawing, pounding, a crying child, cowbells, birds. And more crying. Peeking from under my blindfold I see Fiorenza collapsed in the middle of the floor among the dancers, sobbing. Another woman is huddled with her for comfort. When the music stops for twenty minutes of silent rest, she is still weeping, desperate, but there is a correspondence between her and the others. In some odd way I feel she is weeping for me, for all of us, and although in any other terms or place or time it would be impossible to glorify another's pain, here it seems right. At the end when we disperse and I want to go to her to explain my peculiar gratitude, she is not to be found.

Nor does she return for the Gaurishankar meditation. The group regathered for this one passes insect repellent around—it's twilight and we have the darshan's mosquito overflow to deal with. Breathe in through the nose and hold as long as possible; out through the mouth and hold. The sound is of tom-toms vibrating through the air like a giant's heartbeat, backed by a celestial squeezebox. When the music changes, a strobe light on the stage flashes on and we are meant to stare at it, though only squinting is manageable. The eyes tear with the splashing brilliance of the light, creating distortions of beautiful stalactites and stars. In the third stage, we stand slowly and weave in place or, as the instructions on the wall have it, "Let latihan happen. In latihan, you let the body be soft and loose. . . . Don't you do the moving; let the moving move you." And finally lie down again, in the dark now. The name of this one, Gaurishankar, is the Indian name for Mount Everest, someone says. Why is a meditation called Mount Everest? "Because it's such a high."

There is something strange going on at home: Judith is washing her hair. I have an idea why, but can't face its recognition now.

August 12

Recognize it or not, I couldn't sleep. This morning Judith is too chirrupy to be borne: lots of secret humming, unaccountable Madonna-smile, altogether irritating cheer. The direct question nails down the direct answer Yes, she is taking sannyas tonight; it only steeps me in despair. As it was predicted so it will be: both my friends will leave London now. Of course she says it won't change anything. That's what Dinah said too, even after "Pankaja" was born and gone away.

I trudge along to the discourse sleepy and grumbling and in he comes, the old Bagwash. But he's got a surprise for me, wouldn't you know. "The first question. I have been thinking all day of the way to ask the question. . . ." How amazing, he is answering me.

You cannot stop thinking, he says, it must stop on its own. In fact the effort to force such an end will result in anxiety or madness. It's not that no-mind comes from the deliberate act of stopping the mind: when the mind stops, then there is no-mind.

"So what to do? Your question is relevant." (And my ego grateful.) The point is not to fight yourself and split in two, but to watch. "And don't watch like an enemy: whenever you look at something as an enemy, you never look deep, you avoid. Don't be a fighter, be a lover." The mind is "the masterpiece" and must be seen with love, with respect. Watch it as you would watch clouds cross the sky—and gradually in your witnessing there will come a pause, as between clouds, when one has passed and another has not yet come. Watch these pauses, and they will give you hints of what samadhi is.

Eventually it is possible to become the mind's master. Then it is your instrument, to use or not as the need arises, as you use your limbs. "When I am answering your question I am using the mind: there is no other way; it is a medium to relate. When I am alone, there is no-mind."

This calls to mind a thought that was annoying me all night. Among the thoughts I never had before are the new ones about the dangers of thinking. Having to use his mind in order to have us not use ours, Bhagwan is giving me more thoughts not to think. Is this a contradiction?

He speaks of computer-minds, of drugs (a "violence to the mechanism" whose effects can mimic no-mind—but then they, not you, are your master), of the Jungian collective unconscious, of yoga ("Standing on the head destroys the mind: that is why you never come across a very intelligent yogi"). He compares the mind to a furled flower: if you pull the petals open, far from experiencing its beauty, you just destroy it. The mind must never be treated with violence. He is opposed to violence of all kinds, he says, but most of all violence against the self.

There are other questions; they almost could have been asked by me, and the answers relate to me. Today he is the kindly torturer, comparing us to Buddhas and full of blessing after yesterday's rough "Come out!" He talks of the need to live both as introvert and extravert—just as a bird can fly only with its two opposing wings, a person who is aware must be able to move from the marketplace to the monastery and back, without getting stuck in one place: for that is a "lopsided life." Your outside and your inside are your wings."

There are people who have become fixated in the marketplace and others in the monastery, living entirely in their social lives or in a state of prayer and introspection. Neither, in his view, is the way to understanding. It is necessary to form relationships with all kinds of people and this is enriching and valuable, but when the time comes one must recognize it and relate to the self, too. Go out, he is saying, but in time, come home.

Why can't Dinah go out, Bhagwan? is the thought I am trying to watch now. Why can't you let Dinah out? She has given you her mind, and you are making her decisions now. Why can't she come home to us as well as home to you?

Or is she (leaning on the wall over there, eyes closed) deciding after all, in choosing not to listen? It certainly is there to hear.

But on he goes. The need for balance, a Zen saying: "Walk in the river but don't get your feet wet." Be in the world but not of the world. Then the question of work and the need to rest—the Judaeo-Christian notion of God's toil for six days and rest on the seventh. The Hindus have another idea—leela, or God's play. God, in their view, wouldn't have needed a rest because his very work would have been a rest. In our world we differentiate between a profession and a vocation: a job is a drudge which earns you a holiday; but a hobby needs no rest because your work and play are the same thing. Hear, hear. My friend Jim Haynes calls it Fullering, and suggests we give up the whole dire idea of *work*. Fine for those who can. Bhagwan thinks that anybody can; but isn't his distribution of tasks to those least fitted to do them by skill or inclination a bit like rubbing their noses in it? God may have his leela and Bhagwan may too; I'm worried about the menials around here, both in and out of orange.

However, we have come to the third question. "What is the difference between looking and seeing?" Looking, he replies, is related to searching: you are looking *for* something, a goal whose very existence negates the true search. Looking for truth cannot be done, because the seeker has an a priori concept of his goal and is obliged to satisfy it. If you are looking, don't come to Bhagwan, because you will find nothing but your own idea.

Seeing, on the other hand, is without conditions, has no expectations, carries with it no conclusions. It is simple openness: experiencing, witnessing, silently and fully. You can come to truth only this way, when you have dropped all ideologies, theologies, philosophies, preconceptions: naked as a child.

The talk reverts to the idea of balance, the need to avoid extremes (eating too much and then fasting: "Whenever a society becomes very rich, fasting becomes a cult. It is difficult to find an American woman who is not on a diet") and to keep moving, never to stop anywhere. Whatever you do, avoid *character*. A man of character is no longer free to respond to life; he is constantly buttressing his character, living up to it, protecting it, indulging it. "He is predictable." But full consciousness means treating every instant as the first, as new. "Don't allow your knowing to become knowledge, and never allow your knowledge to create a character for you. A character is an armor, and in the armor you are jailed: you can never be spontaneous."

At the end of the discourse Bhagwan seems to turn around on what he has said, scrutinize it, and realize how hard it seems. He comes as close as he can to apology— acknowledging the difficulty of the course he proposes against the ease of proposing it. "But that is the only way that you can attain to satchitananda, to truth, to consciousness, bliss. Yes, it is hard. One has to pay too much for it. But God is not cheap."

Slowly filing out, a distressed mother makes after-theater conversation with her son. "You gotta hand it to him," she says, as she looks for her shoes in the mound of sandals, "he's sure got charisma."

I have a date in the marketplace with Meera, an Indian graduate student who was once a neighbor in London and returned home to write a thesis on housing for the poor. Her family's house, in a far-off quarter of Poona which the British failed to transmogrify, is neither poor nor very rich but old and full of character (I like this kind of character, whatever he said this morning): its own, Indian, or more specifically Marathi, with few concessions to Occidental "civilization." Rooms have been appended as the need arose, and filled with strange objects chosen for craft and love, not ostentation. In Meera's own room a giant desk and four-poster and armchairs, all carved and polished, and old Rajasthani hangings on the walls. Beneath the stairs a puja cupboard for the daily religious ceremony—a priest comes every morning, she says, because her father is often working in Bombay and her brother is too lazy, and a man must perform it. Her mother serves us an elaborate meal, half a dozen mysterious vegetarian dishes all unlike anything I've ever eaten, but better. When I thank her for her efforts she says it took no time at all, only two or three hours.

After lunch we walk through the streets that seem another city from the Poona Dinah showed me: no English signs, no English dress, no English order. Rich smells and colors and a chaos which makes its own sense. On the pavements vendors squat beside their mounds of chilies, onions, lentils, greens, and roots all piled in neat pyramids. We stop in a bazaar where the booths display different pieces of a goddess. People haggle for the arms here, torso there, the head at a third and, having acquired all the elements, assemble them at home. As I am negotiating for a pair of stuffed yellow arms, each wearing blue glass bracelets, an odd hallooing catches my attention from the dark behind the counter. Drinking tea and grinning in the gloom are the three men who shared my taxi from Bombay. Two million people live in Poona. These three seem like old friends, if we could only speak.

Meera tells me of the shanty towns she visits and the hopelessness of the inhabitants—sometimes they are uprooted forcibly and sent miles away from their work, but there is little chance of moving otherwise. Strangely, the untouchables, the harijans, have more possibilities than the lower castes that are theoretically above them. Committed to no particular place or work or way of life, some harijans have risen to high government posts. But among the three lowest castes—the barbers, the leather workers, and the bhangi, who clear up the shit—there is no mobility because they have the security of their work, however lowly. Others refuse to do these jobs, so they always have a livelihood, and remain inert in it. Shades of poor whites in the U.S. South: The lowest castes are perhaps the most conservative of all in their desire to maintain the system, taking comfort in their "superiority" over the wretched outcastes. The government is trying to shuffle things up by organizing a census in which each family, since few can write, is to be photographed. Later, little do they know, the families so recorded will have to pay fifteen rupees a month ground rent which most cannot possibly afford. The carrot for this operation is the government's promise to render those who cooperate eligible for alternative accommodation, which of course all want. It's a hypothetical carrot, however—there is no alternative accommodation, and no resources to build it.

In a country without work, you often must invent your own. Meera describes the occupations of the shanty people. Women sometimes roll beedies at home, each one tied with a neat red bow, for one rupee per hundred, earning maybe two hundred rupees a month. But many jobs evolve out of scavenging, and people have their own specialties. There is never any rubbish, come to think of it, to be seen. Some collect only rags, which they wash, cut into squares, and sell by the stack to garages. Others find old cigarette packets, clean and press them flat, sell the silver paper to snuff packagers, and cut the cardboard into strips for tapers (each tobacco/betel stall has a tiny oil lamp and a cup of tapers for customers to light the single cigarette that is the usual purchase). There is a big market for used plastic bags for the roofs and raincoats I've seen. We are walking, as Meera talks, just behind a young woman balancing on her head an enormous basket stacked precariously with old tin cans, which Meera supposes she has been collecting all morning. "She finds some but mostly buys them for a few paisas from people's houses. In the shanty town where she lives there are dealers who give her a little profit. The dealer sorts them into ones that are still usable, which he can sell for people to store rice away from the rats, and he employs another man who makes new lids for that. The tins with rust or holes he sells to someone else who flattens them out and resells them to a market stall, where they are sold again to the shanty-town people to nail to the roof." As she talks I'm trying to count how many people have a piece of this action: the person who sells the cans, this woman ahead of us who collects them, the dealer, the lid maker, the rice-and-rat owner, the flattener, the market man, the fellow with the hole in his roof. That makes eight, at least five of them involved in their particular strategy for survival full time, and all because there is no housing, no money, no work to begin with.

Split world: when I get back to the ashram I notice that all the shanties by one building site—where the little boys were doing their toilet yesterday—have totally vanished. There is no question of finding out why. The workers of course are all still there, with their smallest children begging from us at the gate.

I am walking Judith to the death of Judith. She is taking sannyas and will soon be someone else. I'm not sure why, but it doesn't worry me now. After a day outside, these events have their own proportions again. We wait by the gate with the crowd to be smelled, Judith calm and excited at once, and when her name is called for the last time she sails off like a great (clean) boat. Walking home, my sense of felicity passes beyond anything in memory; I can nearly float. For some reason, while I am renewed by this place, I've got another feeling of renewal—or priorities, why I'm here and where my limits are. I love those morning words, but I cannot call a man God. I love this spirit of laughter and dancing of his, but I can't see any of either in the authoritarian gatekeepers and guards who make humorless rings around him. I can't, as well, square the orange and the mala with myself. I don't feel capable of reverence and seriousness for them, or whatever it is they are all giving them. To me it's sacrilege, in the best religious sense, to give this best of religions a symbology that synchronizes with crucifixes and nuns' habits or pais and yarmulkas or the robes of the blond Sufis of Maida Vale. If it isn't in the heart, it isn't in the costume. The important thing is to listen to what Bhagwan says, not to don the symbols and risk feeling safe.

It's strange to hear myself accepted in the same spirit as I accept (and rejected similarly: not being a sannyasin I am Other, Under, Odd to those who are). But when he answered my question today, and even afterward, I had the impossible feeling that his eyes sought me out from the hundreds there; that whenever my head fell and attention wandered he was looking at me to pull me back. It was always true; he always was. (On another level, how can it have been true?) (Does it matter?)

The point is I feel met on my level: That is his talent, magic, or whatever it is. He gives me what I can take. That for me he leaves a lot out has to be accepted too. Any vacuums are beside the point when one confronts him, however powerfully they hit me before and after: not just the feelings of resentment and social pressure from the surrounding sannyasins, but the way all of them omit to mention or to see or care about the horror of the base on which they exist, the beggar children at the gates, the absence of the kind of holiness which extends to charity and justice, those qualities which are the foundations of my concept of religion (bequeathed me by my father, who is strong enough a father to obviate my need of another father now). Neither side is enough by itself (the bird's wings?) but there is an obvious need, it seems to me, for the one to depend on the other—for political and social concerns to be based for their implementation on a structure of peace with and within oneself. I always questioned how my father, who couldn't sort things out with my mother, had the nerve to take on sorting out the world with his radical journalism and speechmaking. And wondered if, were she to achieve a coherent vision of her relationship to the whole independent of men, she could act where now she can only lament. As I am both these people, I am all my own questions about them too.

I am alone in our room. Someone is playing a flute. The desk is covered with ticking clocks to remind us of our meditational duties. Judith (who even now is not Judith) is rejecting her old life as she accepts a new name, a new birthday. August 12. (Will we ever celebrate again at Manzi's? If so, which birthday?) She is welcoming in an existence of what she called (happily) "chaos and pain." Having spent years and a fortune, like so many of the others, in a psychoanalysis designed to come to terms with that very chaos and pain, she is now anxious to reawaken it and work it out all over again. None of them see things as I do, and I suspect only Bhagwan would appreciate (two senses) that. Perhaps he was right about me—or why should I feel so marvelously well, so organically smooth and strong, when all of those in exterior orange are suffering from interior illness and trauma? Maybe I do start out somewhere else. Where?

In any case, I'm happy. Haven't felt able to say that, except in moments gone before they count, for years. Write it down, I am happy. See? It doesn't go away.

Judith returns early in her mala. She left before darshan was over, she says, by improvising a few coughs, because after she had taken sannyas it was all too much for her.

_____ _____

"What's your *name?*" I can't help behaving as though someone's been born.

"Ma Anand Savita." Anand is "bliss." Savita means "source of light," and came with the advice: Attend to the moon. This particularly delights her as the moon rules her sign, she's always had a special affinity for the moon. And: Consider the rose, how it only exists because of the light.

True romance. She can't stop grinning and whirling about. We decide to celebrate with a drink at the Blue Diamond, leaving a note for Pankaja and Devopama. Nobody's on speaking terms even now, so who knows. On the way to the hotel in the dark, Savita—the name, being Latinate, comes easily—tells me more about the row with Pankaja—if I can remember Judith's name, why not Dinah's?—which apparently ended in fisticuffs. She is actually bruised. What it was immediately about is petty, Pankaja complaining about Judith's behavior on the train, her concern with comfort and her beautiful-woman's vanity ("Always worried about your hair. Who cares about your fucking hair"); in fact it has a history of buried rivalry, love, truce, and sources beyond speculation. But Pankaja's attitude is enough to satisfy Savita that their friendship is over. Bunch of melodrama, seems to me. I've seen them at it before, flinging the entire contents of my living room at each other one day, arm-in-arm the next. Talking about it leads to firmer commitments, so leave it alone.

In any case we've barely begun our gin-and-limes when the other two arrive and, as if there'd never been the least antagonism, everybody's kissing and congratulating, we have the story of the rose and moon again, many more gin-and-limes until we're out of rupees, and back home cheerfully enough.

August 13

Do another dynamic in the morning. Establish that
I hate it and will not do it again. Nitpicking
maybe, but I cannot coexist with, let alone abandon myself
to, that "music." It isn't music at all but a violence to the
ear, clashes of cacophonous gongs, locomotive huffing
noises, the drumming of madness—anyway an intrusion,
defining what it wants from me as much as the screams
which drowned it in London. Dinah was let off going by
Bhagwan some time ago, and my reasons are just as good.
Besides, I don't have to do anything. Do I?

Time for a quick breakfast and a dousing with cold
brown water before the discourse. Savita is fretting about
her mala, what a bore it is. "Are you resenting it yet?" a
German mind reader asks. As we file into the hall, a whip-
poorwill is singing from the portico where Bhagwan will sit
in his G-plan swivel chair. The early light shines sideways
through the trees—one that looks as if it's had a hormone
shot with outsize fern leaves and great dangling pods, another with the premature colors of autumn, some baby
evergreens sedately in a row. It is so still, like the center of
the universe. For the people seated on the floor, that is what
it is. When he enters, there is a sort of shuddering among

them. We do not have to think or worry: Bhagwan our spiritual placenta will nourish us again.

"Bhagwan," the soft voice of Teertha comes from nowhere. "There was a man of Wei, Tung Men-wu, who did not grieve when his son died. His wife said to him: 'No one in the world loved his son as much as you did. Why do you not grieve now he is dead?' He answered: 'I had no son, and when I had no son I did not grieve. Now that he is dead it is the same as it was before when I had no son. Why should I grieve over him?' "

The interpretation of this parable comes late in the lecture but affects me like a hearing aid must feel to someone who didn't know she was deaf. Bhagwan talks about mourning as an expression of an incomplete experience: "If you love, then love totally—so nothing remains hanging. Otherwise, that hanging, that incomplete experience, that unlived experience will haunt you." The man of Wei, having loved his son so much, was not beset by leftover guilt, feelings withheld when his son lived, unfinished business— the identifiable ingredients of the grief I have felt over someone's death or absence from me. Taking the Zen story literally, I am consumed with wonder at the realization that, after nine concentrated years, I do not miss my children now, that in fact even if I were to hear I would never see them again I could cope "with sadness but not grief," because our relationship, unlike any other, *is* so here and now —and for Bhagwanian reasons. I surrendered to them, in a moment still vivid to me, five years ago. Until then, since their births in fact, I'd carefully kept preserved away from them a part of myself which I imagined was my reality— you can't have *all* of me, you little buggers, I need *some*thing for myself. They knew it, and they never stopped hammering at the final wall between us. At last one day, faced with the impossibility of further resistance, I gave up.

I had a month's work to do and they had a month's holiday. I knew at the end of the month I would be utterly unable to revive the impulses that stimulated the work now. I looked for help and there was none. Driven finally to Mexico in search of someone who would give me time alone, I found instead by my father's swimming pool the last of my hopes give way. Like my husband, mother, and brother, my father, too, was writing every morning. Eve and Moby couldn't swim. Neither could the servants. If my children were not to drown, I just had to sit there. With this realization, I snapped.

At the time it felt as if I were being torn apart on the rack. But having destroyed myself and given them everything, there wasn't even time to survey the derelict results—for they were suddenly, miraculously returning everything to me. No more wall, no more hammering. They understood! Their love was always unconditional; now mine was too. It was the act of surrender that was necessary. At that instant my greatest torment became my greatest pleasure: motherhood was no longer an activity designed to rob me of my separate identity, it was my identity. A kind of ecstasy descended over me, unlike anything I'd ever known outside of love or creativity. Not that such an end could have been plotted: surrender was, and apparently had to be, almost an act of force.

Listening to Bhagwan tell the story now I see all at once what he *means* by surrender—my inexplicable pantomime has a script, and everyone's part in it is clear. I am in constant mourning, not for the life I live but for truncated life, episodes without appropriate conclusions, people to whom I have never given enough who are snatched off from me by some invisible malfunction of a machine, theirs or some other, before I'd told them what I meant—leaving me sputtering But—! But—! Wait—! to the air with nothing back except a silence too loud to allow sleep.

My ended marriage, for example. It wasn't the end that was so bad but the failures of the thing itself. Bhagwan talks of a woman he knew living in mutual antagonism with her husband, who then died, whereupon the widow spent months in extreme anguish, crying and carrying on—until Bhagwan pointed out that her grief made no sense. What are you crying about? he asked her: what is it precisely that you miss? All that fighting? The dreadful life you had together? And, having thought about it, she was compelled to see that he was right. It isn't that I miss him really, she agreed. What I am so miserable about is that we threw away our chances. Quarreling—what about? I can't even remember! "It is not his death—it is my own missed experience of love."

It occurs to me that if my marriage hadn't ended I would never have been in Poona at all. I'd be stuck on some dumb beach. Everything he says is true. I don't miss the marriage, I miss what wasn't there, especially in the last years. But to see this provides less than a cure. For one thing, Bhagwan says incomplete experiences "cannot be dropped." What can you do with them then, apart from trying never to repeat them? In any case, how can you voluntarily *choose* surrender if there is any validity to my experience with my children? I shall send him more questions tonight.

It's an eclectic talk, but with jabs at the old orthodoxies. He is not interested, he says, in the "nonsense" of Hinduism, Islam, Christianity. The important thing is to be religious without a qualification, to be in harmony with a God who has already accepted you just because you are. And "if you don't like the word *God*, you can drop it. I am not a fanatic about language. You can call it 'the existence,' 'the unknown,' 'the truth,' 'the ultimate,' 'the absolute'—any name will do, X, Y, Z. It is not particular so it cannot have a name, an adjective. It is the universal. It is *that which is.*"

His theme is the accidental and the essential. First among accidentals is the ego and its offspring: reputation, money, power, possessions. The sham of success and riches is best expressed by those who have them: "Nothing fails like success," and there is nothing like riches to show how poor their owner actually is. As for the possession of people— "You are not yours! How can anybody else be yours?" The essential is what is called in Zen the *original face*—"the face you had before you were born, the face that will be there when you are dead. Find out the eternal, don't become attached to the accidental. And all is accidental except your witnessing consciousness."

Bhagwan's version of Buddha's Middle Way: "Renunciation does not mean escaping to a monastery. Because if you escape from the world nothing is going to change; you carry the same mind. *Here* in the world, the house was yours, the wife was yours; *there* the monastery will be yours, the religion will be yours. The 'mine' will persist. It is an inner illusion, an inner dream, an inner sleep. Renunciation means coming to know that you cannot possess anything; not dropping the possessions, but dropping possessiveness: what Gurdjieff calls getting disidentified."

"In the accidental world you have to struggle. In the essential world you have simply to surrender. In the accidental world you have to doubt. In the essential world you simply trust—and this trust is not like belief. Belief is against doubt; trust is simply absence of doubt."

The story he uses to illustrate this is what later stings me most. It concerns a botanist who spotted a new species of flower in an inaccessible valley and, in order to acquire it for study, lowered his little boy down on a rope. Terrified as he watched the child pick the flowers, he called: "Are you okay, my son? Are you not afraid?"

"The son laughed. 'Why should I be afraid?' he said. 'The rope is in my father's hands.' "

I know what he means. All these orange people near me, they know even better. While the allegory is meant to show the quality of trust, it clearly speaks to everyone of Bhagwan's willingness to accept their specific trust in him. I envy them that they can say what the boy said. But not only do I not trust Bhagwan or anyone to hold the rope, I find my very envy, my wish to need it too, despicable, and no reason for taking sannyas. It's as bad as joining the army, or committing crimes because you can't handle life out of jail, or getting married. I would like to be as independent and eclectic as he is himself, finding wisdom and love where I can. I find it in him. But if God is the unknown, the absolute, the universal, X, Y, Z, who is he to call himself God? Yet all day the phrase returns like something undigested: "The rope is in my father's hands."

When he finally says "Enough for today" and is gone, it's a shock as if a life were ending and another starting. I've been in a timeless place, with no discomfort on the hard marble. The others, too, in their awkward Western squats and half-lotuses—many haven't moved at all. Now the boy beside me flings his face to the floor, hands outstretched in silent adoration, while others touch the place where Bhagwan's feet just trod. For the very reason that the ideas in the talk today struck me so hard, their reactions are upsetting, because their insistence on the man as living icon removes him from our access. If God is speaking, how can mortals take his ideas for themselves? They are as beyond us as the kingdom of heaven he wishes us to discard along with our old "religions." As he said today (free translation), renunciation of one's possessions is meaningless when one then possesses the very act of renunciation: possession is a state of mind. The more recent converts—like any converts—are the best demonstrations of this. They cherish their soul's discoveries as my son does his new bicycle. Worship is as much a state of mind as possession. If you need a god, you'll always find one. But worship creates its own caste system in the distinction between the worshiped and the worshiper, and removes from human possibility the example of the deified. As safe as the boy on the end of the rope is the one who imagines that he need not try to be as his God is, because he cannot. The next step is: It's sacrilege to try. So how can Bhagwan say "You don't need to use the word *God*" and use it about himself in Sanskrit? How can he claim trust, not belief, to be the goal and then allow them to believe in him? Blind faith is dangerous, and the frills of orange and mala—not to mention the ashram's eccentric rituals, from the Gaurishankar meditation to the ultimate hair wash—engender faith, not trust. I want to see what is essential in him, using his own terms, not what is accidental.

The isolation in which these thoughts exist is hardest to bear. Because he is opposed to thought at all instead of the intuitive leap, I can't talk to him; I can't talk to the committed; I can't find Karen and there isn't anyone else. No context therefore for my questions, no way to tell how realistic, answerable, relevant any of them are, or if I'm only being defensively argumentative. Most sannyasins I talk to condemn me on the latter grounds, implicitly or explicitly; those who don't simply *pity* me (with a patronage that would be funny if it weren't so crippling) or give sanctimonious "advice" based on their superior "insights." Only Dinah can absorb it, listen, often agree, but finally give the impression that it's all beside the point as far as she's concerned. But Dinah is not only politic; Dinah is Dinah. She is more a reference point in the universe than almost anyone I know, she is of the lament, "I don't know who I am." And yet her early irreverence is disappearing in a startling loss of humor, both good and sense of.

Now she is quite Pankaja, returning with me to the ashram for a siesta to today's tape. First, a detour to a room in one of the residences above the meditation hall, where two Englishwomen live in a small cubicle made spacious by their artful carpentry. They work for their places: one cleans the smooth stone floor where we sit each morning; one is editing old Bhagwan pronunciamentos for a darshan book, including a tape of the session in which Pankaja consulted him about her children when they wanted to go home. She wants to see again what he actually said.

Reading the manuscript over her shoulder I can grasp the force of his reasoning more clearly than through her summary. He didn't tell her what to do, indeed maintained he shouldn't, for the same reason that he thought she should not impose her ideas on the children. "It is always better to listen to their feelings rather than to your ideas of happiness, because nobody can decide for anybody else what is going to be happiness. . . . Each parent is doing this nonsense to children, and they are never forgiven . . . and nobody can tell them [parents] because they are so loving —that's the trouble. Behind love, so much that is not love goes on hiding."

As to whether she should return with them, the same answer applies: "If you feel like going, it is for your happiness; or if you remain here, it is for your happiness. Otherwise you will not be able to forgive them, and for your whole life you will be saying that you wanted to be in India but because of them you are there."

His point is easy to see—but was it enough? What about responsibility? Is there such a thing in his scheme of things, to anyone but the (egoless) self? Mothers shouldn't have to sacrifice their happiness nor children theirs, but what of the children's need for their mother? After all, they were only ten. How could they be expected to take complicated decisions which in effect made their happiness subject to long division? If he simply had acknowledged these points, it seems to me her decision might have been different. For all his approval of adult-as-child, however, he doesn't seem to have time for the child-as-child. As it was, I can see how guilt-producing his remarks would have been to me, and she seems to suffer a revival of her own in reading them.

But later, having wrong thoughts while humming, I can understand how right he was too, as far as he went, from my experience. How I always unquestioningly admired my father for doing what he had to do, despite its attendant neglect of us (obvious to everyone but me), and resented my mother for trimming her sails and nobly sacrificing herself for our "happiness." (It's just as easy to see that I'm probably guilty of the same thing with my children; in fact who's to say that what I impose on them can even be dignified by the name happiness?) What I dislike about Bhagwan's nondirective—his final advice to Dinah was "If you cannot decide, consult the I Ching!"—is the blackmail implicit in the idea that parents "are never forgiven," that the children will hate you in the end. Maybe they will, maybe they won't, but it's not a basis for action or a justification for none; nor indeed is there a "they," a "children" as some general category rather than three distinct people, with only one of whom was he familiar.

There are perceptibly fewer thoughts among the meditations as the days go by. In the kundalini, especially, I lose myself. I'm making strides in Being Aware. Whatever I am doing: Stop. Be. Feel. It's a great pleasure, rather akin to an extended brown study from which you feel no urge to snap out—though a tiny question occasionally subverts my efforts. It has to do with hemispheres of the brain. The left, they say, takes care of linguistic, cognitive, organized thought, while the right is largely reserved for emotion, intuition, sensuality. Little doubt remains about the Master's values in this split. When I am in a beatific trance of Awareness, it is hardly an intellectual matter. Is this what it's like to have a stroke?

When Eve said "Don't get hypnotized," she had a point. I rally my resources and yet nothing outside Bhagwan interests me anymore. I'm in a funny limbo, tend to disremember how I used to keep my balance in the long-gone days two weeks ago before this swami got to be my substitute for gravity. Read a piece about hypnotizing chickens: "Seize it firmly and hold it on its side on a flat place for half a minute or so, by which time it should have become completely inert. Traditionally, you then convince it that it is tethered to the earth by drawing a chalk line from the tip of its beak, but this is an unnecessary refinement. Depending on the chicken, it could stay immobilized for a couple of hours before coming to with a few squawks and walking off." A chicken can squawk and forget it. The problem with Poona is whether one comes to, and if so, to what.

We all have mesmerizing experiences. Orators to oracles use the same techniques and mostly people fall for them. So many humdrum jobs are matters of routine, soon performed with trancelike rhythm. Much of any love affair is mutual hypnosis: the stronger need or personality convincing the weaker to relinquish control, and everybody happy about it; or more equally a complicit exchange—taking turns—of some degree of your autonomy. You meet someone you trust, you give some soul. It's hard to resist trusting Bhagwan, especially if the weight of the responsibility of coping with self and life is too great to bear, and he so obviously responds, cares, and can bear it for you. You invest in him all the good that has ever surrounded the good in yourself, and you feel you are working with him *as a team* to root out in you the egotistic, earthbound, smelly unperson which causes all the guilt and pain. The daily discourses act to hold the chicken firmly on its side, and other reinforcements are constantly available: the taped lectures, his ubiquitous picture, his lieutenants and other surrogates pushing and pulling at you, groups to provide the feeling of progress and productive growth, and above and around it all, this strange concept of Bhagwan's "energy"—his field which these followers have sacrificed their lives to enter. And then there is the orange and the mala, not just symbols of subjugation to the outside world but a felt weight about the neck, a perceived flash of color in the eye. (The sensory gap is aural: There ought to be a theme song to play back in the mind's ear. But to fill the sound void there is The Voice.) Much of it is as unnecessary as the chalk line from the chicken's beak. Sannyasins are willingly tethered without such illusions. They are devoted to Bhagwan, enslaved to him, surrounded and surrendered—not to his philosophy, but to him. This provides a clue to the existence here of the hypnotic state in general: the great difficulty of coherently, persuasively reproducing his ideas, as distinct from their delivery. Separating out the style from the content, something unsatisfactory is left. Strangers are singularly unimpressed by reading the newsletter or hearing a tape. It's the show, the aura of the man that does it. Rather than a particular Bhagwanian philosophy, there are a lot of well-tried and true ideas delivered by a *very strong personality*.

One of the chief strengths of this personality lies in its paradoxical ability to convince the converted that it doesn't exist at all. Since the worst sin is ego, Bhagwan can't have any. Sannyasins are meant to "drop" theirs too, in the process of surrendering to him. And yet it is a puzzle: What is most pampered and catered for in Poona, if not the ego? One is urged, compelled to enter into a deep, prolonged course of self-study, self-reflection, self-improvement (without, however, being permitted use of the one tool which might endow the rest with value: independence of judgment). You are supposed to love yourself but only if you love Bhagwan better, surrendering your ideas about yourself in deference to his. You are encouraged to believe that you, too, are God, but it's a theoretical belief merely, as it is allowed no expression which conflicts with the official precedents: Bhagwan is Goddest (Laxmi, Teertha, & Co. being definitely Godder).

Doublespeak, hypocrisy. A man is called God. Having forsworn ego, he strives egolessly to combat the ego in others. The dreaded ego's first residence, he says, is the body and its glorification. But he encourages his followers to worship his image. He poses for new photographs wearing all kinds of funny hats (How could God be bald?). He despises the poor and his own countrymen. His catchy showbiz humor constantly betrays him. Rather than be caught out by any criticism, he calls his behavior deliberate, a joke or a test or a trick. How can he lose? Simply by allowing himself to be called God, he inspires the double-edged perception that, while God would never do such a thing, who but God would have the gall?

Alone in the bungalow reading the Master: a published collection of darshan tapes. I am copying out some remarks of his on the question of insanity. "This is one of the most significant things to understand: Almost 90 percent of the people who are in madhouses are not mad. They are just playing a role, because people have forced that role on them, and they accepted it. They find it comfortable and convenient, and once they accepted it, it doesn't look good to destroy people's expectations. This is my understanding: If you say to a hundred mad people that they are not mad, ninety can come out immediately—if they are allowed to come out, and if they are made to understand that they are just playing a game. And it is a foolish game, because they are the losers."

A knock on the door: a young sannyasin who has an appointment with Savita. I invite her to wait in our room and offer a drink. Asked how she knew Judith, she says they met in London when she was a resident at Portland Road, one of Laing's Philadelphia Association "asylums." I know the place. Judith asked me to go there once to take a shift with a woman who was so frenetically crazy that she had exhausted everyone to the point of craziness themselves; but when I arrived she had "flown the coop" as they eventually bothered to tell me—"they" being a collection of people in such advanced stages of disorientation that for some time I'd wondered who among them was the subject of my visit. Therapists and patients—in the P.A. the distinction between them is not always easy to find and the terms never used anyway. The house was filthy, full of broken furniture and unwashed dishes and decorated with deranged murals done with soap, food, or whatever else had been handy. A guided tour was unlikely. I'd sat there a while, established it was pointless, left.

It seems weird that this woman should come just as I was writing out that passage of Bhagwan's—so close in approach to Laing—and I show it to her. She smiles in recognition, saying it could have been her story: "I'm one of the ninety percent." After successions of institutions she had lived in the same P.A. house for more than two years, fairly stable part of the time but with recurrent psychotic breakdowns. Now, after a year in Poona, she feels well. She certainly seems well. "It's really only just now that I'm sure, too. When I woke up yesterday a friend in my house said to me, 'You know? I think the beast is really out of you!' Then

I had darshan last night and Bhagwan agreed. He said, 'Now let's have no more madness games from you!' " She imitates his singsong accent and admonishing finger, giving a big, open laugh. We have another drink—how delicious, she says, and it's the first she's had in a year. Savita tells me later that she used to be an alcoholic and is horrified I served the gin. But even if I had known, she can now obviously take care of herself. Perhaps she found in Bhagwan someone to assume the ultimate responsibility, within which she can be responsible herself.

What the ashram seems to offer, in fact, is what the Philadelphia Association talks about—an asylum in the sense of a completely protected environment in which to let go. Your father is holding the rope. You will be cared for; you must only trust him completely to catch the pieces when you fall apart. *When*, not *if*? Should you not start out a mess, is becoming one inevitable? How can they make you better if you don't get worse first? The homeopathic cure to life itself? Judith seemed to be saying as much en route to becoming Savita, in choosing her chaos and pain. Maybe if a general despair reaches the point of my specific agony with my children, then a general surrender is needed and possible here: welcomed, even required. My problem is that I still have hope and optimism. But in this company they may not last. There is an apparent conspiracy to convince me that optimism is illusory, fraudulent (viz. Judith's rounding on me for "putting over" the idea that I'm all right). Hopes aren't here/now, are they? And my here/now is often such a risky place, not only populated with starving people but full of personal land mines like this question of pregnancy—believed less and less for lack of another symptom, but still lurking under life with a dull throb, psychically resembling the physical ache in my gum where a wisdom tooth was extracted before I left home. Besides, one of the favorite formulas for deriding the intransigent here is the comment: "She says she doesn't *need* it!" What a hopeless and absurd conundrum—to be made to feel inadequate for feeling adequate.

August 14

The kinds of questions he chooses to answer this morning lend themselves to frivolous, immodest discourse. How do I know she loves me? Why is your aura white, not many colors? (White is all colors, dummy, and an excuse for an elementary physics lesson.) Why do you refer to God as He not She? (Since God is indisputably feminine, goes the answer, the least we can do is *call* Him He.) (To console Him for the insult, I suppose.) Some frightful jokes, one involving a woman barging into an Italian's hotel room and ultimately his bed on a series of pretexts built on "You don't know me, I don't know you, but . . ." etc., quite unmemorable. Another joke which is disgustingly anti-Semitic, but I suppose Bhagwan's meant to be above all that. A couple of tigers are walking through the woods, when the second tiger pokes his nose in the first one's ass. First tiger: "What's the matter with you, you have the hots for me or something?" Second Tiger: "No, but I just ate a Jew and I need to get the taste out of my mouth."

Every discourse has its jokes, read off the slips of paper Bhagwan brings in with him. Usually they're prefaced with "I have heard . . ." You couldn't call them humor, though the faithful go to pieces with these gags. I am reminded of my lifelong problem with Indians: We don't seem to laugh at the same things. Of all amusements, an Indian being funny amuses me least.

Perhaps Bhagwan is trying to bridge the gap between the hardy-har-har jokester mentality of the West and his own inscrutably giggling countrymen. His jokes are certainly jarring. They seem to come from somewhere else. Indeed they do, Dinah explains—sannyasins contribute them regularly from all over the world. They constitute an intentional shock, she says—because a moment of release in laughter lowers all defenses, opening the way in, too. To me these raucous stories intrude on his tranquillity like a plane above a calm sea cracking the sound barrier.

If anything, today's performance goes to show Bhagwan's human after all. Wish I weren't so disappointed. But there's so little time left, and none to squander on this stupidity. Judith and I had both submitted sad, serious questions which couldn't have been further from his mood. I still want to know his views on dropping an incomplete experience. Or how to "drop" anything. The metaphor is photographic: a little girl holding a ball, a lovely red ball, or is it a tumor? But there it goes, she *drops* it, plunky-plunk-plunk, off it rolls, safely disappearing through the hedge, all gone. It is dropped. And I see Fiorenza, who appears to have dropped everything.

When she talks later about why she cried the other day, she explains it had to do with old but freshly reopened wounds—and she seems freer now for having purged herself. In fact it's inappropriate to pursue, she is lit *up*. Constantly in animated conversation with responding people, exuding love, so nice. Makes me feel intolerably lonely. I go to sulk behind a palm tree.

Matters are not improved by a gregarious American wearing an old-style mala who approaches me with an unprecedented friendliness. Upon establishing my situation—not only that I've just arrived but am soon leaving—he looks aghast at the idea that I came for the camp but will miss the groups. I cannot gather what exactly is the problem until he asks, "But didn't you get laid?"

Eh?

"Well for God's sake, baby, what do you think the groups are for? You mean to tell me you haven't got laid?" he repeats disbelievingly. "At *all?*"

"Afraid not."

"But why do you think people *come* here?"

I say that wasn't why *I* had come here. With a look of helpless commiseration not unlike the one that others have for my spiritual inadequacies, "Outasight," he mumbles, and soon is.

Just then I see an unbearably orange Karen. She is wearing an idiotic grin above her mala. "What happened to you?" I ask, trying not to let my outrage show.

"I'm so *high,*" she croons. "I'm flying. The second I saw him I knew. Make the leap! Right! What about you? It's beautiful. Listen, forget all that stuff I said. This is it! This is really *the trip!*"

I didn't ask whose name.

There is no help from Pankaja, still indistractibly twiddling her hair into plaits and stubbing out beedies on her armchair, writing her journal for Bhagwan. Devopama is not happy either, but whatever is happening between them is not broadcast. Meanwhile I mention to him what the American said in the garden, expecting some support for my surprise. But Devopama is only surprised at me. "What do you think the kundalini is all about?" he says.

"What the kundalini is all about?"

"Of course. All that shaking. It's an audition, how you'd do in bed. Everyone goes to it to find lovers. Even the old ashram people go."

The kundalini is the only meditation I've ended up enjoying. I was auditioning? Failed, then.

One blow follows another. Savita announces that she wants to extend her stay here beyond mine and needs to change her flight reservation. The plan is to put off the patients in letters she will send with me. The patients have pretty well left her mind. I wonder if they will return. Apparently Bhagwan said to her: "*We have some unfinished karma together.*" She has not told me this; word spread from someone else at her sannyas-darshan. It is not the sort of remark he has been known to make before ("Hea-vy"). The stakes are rising.

We go to town, Savita and Fiorenza and I, to a café to wait for Moses the ticket fixer. You can't book international flights from Poona, and rather than waste a day in Bombay everybody relies on this mythic personage who turns up twice a week to convey their latest travel notions to the right computers for a fee which, while extortionate, hardly compares with the loss of a day's spiritual discovery. This café is dishearteningly crowded with customers in orange regalia when we arrive, and as we wait half an hour for a mere pot of tea, I count how long it all may take if everyone gets his quota of Moses. I've already toted it into the day after tomorrow by the time the rumor passes around the room that the man won't be coming anyway.

The monsoon clouds are crouching low and look about to explode any moment all the morning. I want to call today off. Noted in passing: Hotel 7 Loves, Hotel Goodluck, Love Nest Permit Bar, Try Luck Cafe, Help of God Restaurant.

August 15

"The only way to come home is to surrender." As for me, I'm rather busy washing my hair. Thinking: If you *must* go all the way through an experience to surrender, who knows but that hair washing might be my route? Remembering: A Zen story Bhagwan told this morning, about a champion wrestler who kept losing to amateurs despite his prowess, until he spent a night watching the waves and understanding in their constancy the source of their power. And "Call it God, call it the whole. To fight it is to be like a leaf that fights the tree."

He's always putting emphasis on innocence, the childlike surrender. *But a real innocent would have surrendered to so many other forces on the way to you* (I am talking to Bhagwan again, not unusual these days) *that he might never have arrived. I know you say the world is full of phony gurus: How can we evaluate without the rationality you'd have us drop? One can't always just feel who is right; everything's become too packaged for the instant recognition of what's real. Besides, people who surrender blindly not only always have, they will again—away from you, first chance they get.*

Better wash my hair again.

My appetite at lunch is somewhat inhibited by the view this morning of Clara chopping the vegetables on the floor not far from a neatly swept heap of rat turds. Luckily for once there is some dialogue for distraction.

First German (male) to Second German (female): "Did you scream this morning?"

Second German: (Very long silence) "Mm."

First German: "'I thought it was you. Rolfing?"

Second G: (Equally long silence) "Mm." (Second German, taciturn at the best of times, is the one who just spent the week with the SILENCE notice pinned to her robe and is perhaps out of practice.)

First G: "What's he doing?"

Second G: (resigned) "Trying to separate my muscles and scrape things off my bones."

Dane: "If you didn't resist, it wouldn't hurt."

Pankaja: "If she didn't resist, she wouldn't need it."

Second G: "Anyway it's impossible to resist, you have to have all your energy just to bear it."

No thanks.

Some of yesterday's doubts are cleared up in a gossip about Bhagwan's sex life. The visible duties of Vivek, the shakti, are to dispense malas and to sit propped against a special bit of wall during the discourses. She looks so constantly down-at-the-mouth that she appears to be consciously illustrating his answer to the recent audacious question "What do you do with Vivek?"—"Destroy her." After some initial shock people took him to mean her ego. More concretely, everyone is furiously curious about her functions, apart from the special cooking she apparently does for him. Savita says she heard that they sleep in the same bed but "no one knows if they do anything anymore." Bhagwan's alleged sexual transcendence has made this goal top priority for everyone. To this end one must, of course, go all the way through it; so many of the groups are devoted to sexual activity of a varied and imaginative kind. Transcendence is seen in male terms, I gather: What appears to be out is the masculine version of coming. Sounds pretty yogic to me—don't let the women get your sacred bindu. On the other hand, what purpose would it serve anyway, since children are considered so objectionable here you can hardly believe that everybody was one once. The nicest part of the Vivek story, in any case, is the mundane sentimentality of the courtship. It is said that soon after she arrived from England (with a boyfriend) Bhagwan began to send her flowers, little notes. It can't have taken long for her to succumb. Even the boyfriend is still around.

Washing my hair again after lunch, I go outside to dry. Second German is listening to a Bhagwan tape in the curtained-off space that is her room. We're surrounded with the voice: on the veranda Devopama is repeatedly playing another tape of an old discourse in which Pankaja asked the question: "Sometimes I feel I don't exist. When I go into a room no one sees me; when I speak, no one hears. When a friend touches me, I am not solid. I feel like a piece of quicksilver that runs away from between your fingers. How can I lose myself if I am not there?"

A train shrieking down the way is competing with yet another train embalmed on tape, so Devopama has his ear screwed to the speaker. "Nobody can see you except yourself," the voice replies. "They can see your body, your eyes, face, but not you. You are hidden deep behind; these are all curtains. The innermost core is absolutely private. Even lovers cannot penetrate it: That is their misery." (Devopama's?) "Consciousness is an infinite inwardness. If someone can see you, you are reduced to an object. That's why when someone stares at you you feel uneasy."

In a curious aside, Bhagwan explains the Hindus have a

special word for "one who stares too long," and even define "too long" as three seconds. "More than that, you are trespassing, it is a violence." And discusses the treatment of servants and prostitutes as commodities. I take great exception to: "The ugliest woman is more beautiful than the most beautiful prostitute," but the tape spins on regardless. "Feel blessed that nobody can see you, even if they bring magnifying glasses." From the Upanishads: " 'The knower cannot be known, the seer cannot be seen.' People come to me and ask how to see God: foolish people. Not even human consciousness has been seen; how can you see the consciousness of the whole?"

Same for touching. "All that can be touched is not you. The body is flowing. Neither is the mind solid. But you— you are not a flux, you are not a changing phenomenon, you are eternity. You transcend all categories, you are just space, and out of that emptiness all these flowers flower. You are flowers of emptiness, forms of nothingness. That's what we mean when we say God has no forms, but you are all his forms."

I must say that I would find this not only impenetrable but perhaps not worth trying to penetrate if I hadn't experienced what he says in an acid trip. And I wonder—criticize drugs though he may—how many sannyasins came that route. He appeals to the same mentality as does Castaneda, and to the same people who, having experienced chemical ecstasy, the temporary plug-in to the whole, not only understand the terms of reference but sometimes are impelled to track the permanent high. I wouldn't wonder but that many sannyasins have found their Don Juan in Bhagwan. Would this have made as much sense to them earlier? (Maybe he *did* choose the right time to be reborn.)

He returns to Pankaja now, and her specific question. As so often with the doubts of his followers, he rearranges the problem to find a solution (if not the one originally solicited). " 'How can I lose myself if I am not here?' " he quotes her question back to her. "Just to understand this is to lose yourself." No, she is not here, because the "I" that she believes herself to be is not the true "I" but simply the "I" beheld by others—and it is important not to identify with this view of witnesses, not to submit to this objectification of you, but through meditation to reach "the point where you can fall into your own subjectivity, where you can disappear into your own depth, where you can come to realize that which is abiding in you," and has no relation to the ego or to public masks.

"Drop that which you are not so that you can know that which you are. My whole teaching is just to drop that which you are not. It looks paradoxical: I am telling you to renounce that which you don't have. Throw away that which you don't have, so that which you are can become manifested to you, can be revealed to you."

"The second question" comes next, signal for Devopama to rewind the tape to play the answer to Pankaja again. Sitting with him briefly, I am reprimanded for my cigarette because "the smoke will stink up your hair." A dispute arises: Do I smell or not. The only answer is another shower at the ashram. Any question about whether the "I" that I think I am is the "I" I am washing will soon be moot, as most of it is disappearing down various drains.

I'm struck on the walk back home by one of those moments when everything is so out of my context that I can only believe I am not here at all: the sensation of dream-within-dream that prompts you to try to wake up. I see someone like me, waterlogged and covered with towels, trudging down a dirt road in India. An electrocuted bat is hanging from a cable overhead. There, approaching, is a pimply youth in a long orange dress. As we meet, he speaks with a strong Teutonic accent: "It's just before kundalini now." "Yes," I answer, "but I have darshan." We continue on our way.

What *is* all this? Which playwright-in-the-sky devised such dialogue? What is who doing in this place? I am a letter addressed to The Occupant. Tell me who is there! Two weeks ago I was a normal person. To the extent that I know what Dinah's question to Bhagwan meant, I don't feel answered. To the extent that I understand the answer, there is no question.

Savita has cunningly knotted a cotton stole around my arms to protect them from mosquitoes (since after my last insecticideless foray into the night you could hardly see the arms for bites) and keeps me company at the gate of Bhagwan's house to wait for darshan. I just DARE them to stop me. Nobody's ever smelled less than I do. Lots of people today. An Italian family, a quattrocento madonna with child and attendant Joseph, are waiting with their halos polished. And Fiorenza, breathless to discover who she really is. Yesterday she almost got cold feet when she learned she was supposed to wear orange *all the time,* but presumably it's been assimilated by now into her unearthly joy.

"Discovering who you really are"—acquiring the new name and the personality-diagnosis it seems to represent—has another auto-voyeuristic dimension beyond the merely personal. The "family" name (Deva, Anand, Yoga, Prem, etc., which follows "Ma" or "Swami" and precedes the individual name) came up for discussion over dinner. An American (who was not introduced) plunged into a good tongue-wag about some people unknown to me. A tale of a first encounter had as sauce, "I just *knew* he was an Anand the second I laid eyes on him! They're so—essential, you know?" The said Anand's "old lady" was, however, a Prem.

"Those Prems! I can tell one anywhere." The American frowned knowingly, until Prem Pankaja objected. "Oh it's not like *bad* or anything, it's just my karma," was the answer. "I have this thing with Prems," he said. The dialogue was sounding more and more familiar, and I was grateful to the American for pinning down why. "It's like when I was a Taurus. I had this fatal attraction to Scorpios, and every time it was like horrendous." (The new birthdays are presumably extrahoroscopic.)

Shiva appears and intones the rules, we are summoned and smelled. I am passed—but they swipe my stole, intolerably mean. The madonna, halo notwithstanding, is refused admission on grounds of eau de cologne, and the family confronts one another at the fence with fingers twined through the wire as if unable to part. But they do not quarrel with the decision, unlike two borderline cases who receive the grace of entrance after scarves are hastily found for their heads—one of them my stole, which is a bit much.

These matters seem trivial when Bhagwan is there. In his presence I feel utterly relieved—of doubts, of all the thoughts he'd have me jettison, of anything but gladness, honor. I have no idea what an enlightened master is, but if there is such a thing I am willing to believe he is it. How have I become so persuaded? The steps don't matter anymore. It seems as remarkable as the discovery of a new continent, to encounter such a man in one's life. I think of friends in London who follow Gurdjieff, and pity them that their master is dead. His power was such that it's transcended him. Disciples preach it, the printed word perpetuates it. But Gurdjieff's words are very much the same as Bhagwan's, inevitably: Such wisdom is universal. And I am seeing it *alive*.

Being aware and in the present is complicated by the fact that some moments are longer, fuller, and more important than others. The ones that are full to spilling over tend to do so, into quiet times. Certain people dominate; Bhagwan overwhelms. He absorbs even other people's ideas into his own substance. They say his library is enormous and that he gets through half a dozen books a day. He seems to be able to resurrect the ideas without repetitiveness, and while he always gets quotations wrong, the sense is rendered precisely enough. Of the many subjects he discusses, he *is* all of them and has immediate, spontaneous access to them. I don't really know what he means by ego, but some form of personal intervention is missing in him. There is an old Zen game I've played for years: When I throw a piece of paper into the basket across my kitchen, it only lands inside if *it* is meant to, not if *I* am putting it there. With him, it always seems to land inside.

He is naming disciples the way kings dub knights. The first means "Divine Dimension" which is the "capacity to feel the presence of God everywhere;" the second is "Swami Prem Nadam": "Prem means love and Nadam means the subtlest sound: the sound of love." When he gets to Fiorenza she gives me a sideways farewell and slides forward. Bhagwan bids her close her eyes and relax: "I am going to shake you to the very foundations!" whereupon she falls before him in a fetal position, while he studies her and cogitates. He writes and writes on his clipboard, and then he calls her "Ma Deva Yama": Divine Night. "Your time is the night." She sits attentively again as he elaborates.

Yoga psychology, he says, distinguishes four stages of human consciousness. The first is the normal waking state in which we conduct our daytime working lives. The second is the dream state: "You are asleep, but dreams are running like a procession. The whole mind is in a traffic jam." Third is deep and dreamless sleep. The fourth, it turns out, is the great aim: samadhi. He says it is as deep as sleep and yet alert at the same time, as silent as sleep but wholly conscious.

Ma Deva Yama seems to find this fourth category as novel as I do, but is clearly ready to start the pilgrimage. She is advised to meditate at night. "Become an owl, mm?"

When he asks if she has anything to say, she tumbles out her sorrows, condensing years of pain to present to him. I can only hear her intermittently, but the replies have satisfied her: when she resumes her place beside me it is with a smile that is divine.

From what I heard, the old fortune teller was at work again, dispensing advice which is applicable, and probably of instant relevance, to anyone. A poet, he can take individuals and turn them—pop!—into generalities. "Never decide for security, otherwise you will always decide wrongly. Always decide for love . . . you need something more, something more ecstatic, to live. When you decide for security, you are deciding out of fear, and when you decide out of fear, you enhance fear, you feed fear. Who cares about security if there is love?"

But first, strength is necessary: the capacity to be alone. Be yourself, and be independent: learning to be alone is a precondition for learning to be happy with another. Two people who cannot be content separately will be even less content together, because they reflect each other's unhappiness and multiply it. "That's what is driving the whole world crazy."

He passes through an odd moment of apparent regret, paraphrasing Shaw on youth being too good to waste on young people. Youth should come when one can take advantage of it, after one has learned how easy it is to destroy love. "By the time a person comes to know, life is gone." But Yama is obviously still full of energy and can fall in love again. What is important is to remain capable of love —it is the appetite which counts, not its satisfaction. But never betray love.

And remain insecure. You can choose the safe life and all it will achieve you is a dull death. "That's what security is. It is a convenient way to live and a convenient way to die. . . . So if you ask me, my suggestion is—live danger-ously. If you were asking for my support, you have asked the wrong man."

A British student named Charles will be reintroducing himself tomorrow as Swami Anand Dheeresh: Bliss and Wisdom. The way of wisdom, he is told, has nothing to do with knowledge. Knowledge is the borrowed wisdom of others: it may look right, but it is counterfeit. Learned men in universities talk about the stars but "they have not even taken the trouble to look *up*." A Christian may memorize the Scriptures but he cannot understand Christian wisdom without becoming a Christ. Wisdom wells out of your own understanding. "And unless something is *yours*, it is worth-less. If something is not yours, drop it. . . . Don't make your being a junkyard."

The new swami, somewhat confused but extremely eager to please, wants to know, on the basis of what Bhagwan has told him, if he should drop out of university? That will not be necessary, Bhagwan consoles him. "But don't become a pundit!"

Two Germans. A sannyasin who complains of "feeling like a skinny devil" is inspirited to hear that he is simply confronting parts of himself that he had repressed; that he should welcome, indeed particularly invite the skinny one, embrace and "absorb your devils. . . . A saint is monot-onous, a sinner also, but a perfect man is both."

A ravishing blond boy of 14, the son of a sannyasin, comes forward and, speaking through an interpreter, frets that "I hide my feelings behind my mind." Bhagwan is sad-dened for him: feeling makes up ninety-five percent of life, he says. Otherwise one might as well be replaced by a com-puter, which is more efficient at thinking anyway. Thinking is mechanical and dead; all that is rich and beautiful comes through feeling. "Feeling makes man a man" and until he realizes this, he will miss his life. Bhagwan prescribes meditation and a Tathata group: this, apparently, is all about feelings and their acknowledgment. "When twenty persons are bringing their feelings out, one simply looks foolish if one is not. . . . You need a little madness, that's all."

While others laugh at this the boy, as he has throughout, keeps his level, solemn gaze on Bhagwan, who is clearly dazzled by him. "You are such a beautiful person," he says. It is nice to know he is not immune to such considerations.

A Dutchman named Hans gets Bhagwan talking politically, a rare event. Ecology is Hans' main interest, and Bhagwan's approval is tempered with caution to take care of "the inner ecology" too. The trouble with the world is the trouble with the individual writ large: People are at war with themselves, each man a mob reflecting his personal disturbance on everything he touches. We are ruled by violent fanatics and always have been—"a peace-loving person does not bother to rule anybody." Ambitious men who are concerned only with their own aggrandizement, the politicians are insane and at this point may easily take us to catastrophe. It is some kind of miracle that Nixon did not destroy us all on his way out. War and the impulse toward it still hold sway. Most of man's creations have been accomplished with war as their purpose; other uses come only later. Roads are not built for lovers to meet, but for armies to pass. Given these basic problems, it is foolhardy to hope too much but still important to go on working: Eventually perhaps we will learn. "The work is good and beautiful and religious. But don't forget yourself."

Vivek's pile of malas has diminished until only one is left. I have been wondering if it was meant for me. But Hans decides spontaneously, the way Bhagwan likes, to become a sannyasin and then there are none. He is called Swami Ramakrishna Paramahansa—the name of the Bengali saint so revered at the Home Science College. "One of the greatest men ever born," says Bhagwan. "Will it be easy to pronounce?"

In a way I'm glad the malas are all gone. I yearn to give in. How marvelous it would be to be among the sannyasins! The comfort and the symmetry of life where everyone must fall in line like filings magnetized. You wouldn't wake up then to such doubt, the sort derived from individual responsibility constantly mutating into new confusions, but able to relax into the infantilism of a calm, coherent, regimented life. You simply *are*, here, part of a complex but ultimately simple scheme, not buffeted about in your own moodiness but driven by the wind and bending to it as the rest, because it's stronger than all others. An end to the terrible need to choose.

There's more to it than that. There is being in a movement again. There is that spirit here of glorious cause. Marching against the bomb, singing for civil rights, working to end the Vietnam War. How many of the people in those movements, or their heirs, sit around me now? Joining in a great movement for change is the source of such absolute exhilaration. We are without a movement in this world now; then why not a movement out of this world? Does it matter what the goals are, as long as you believe in them? (Yes, but let's not go into that.) Where I live, the best that can be said is that they still leave you alone if you're the right color and you don't make waves. It can't last long. Since Bhagwan, far from making waves, deliberately exhorts you to flow with the current, perhaps it's even salutary as a siphon for the discontented energies of the young— who otherwise might find no expression but to make a bomb or organize a terrorist cell (activities which may result in the loss at last of the chance for anyone to be left alone).

But if Bhagwan is doing the West a favor, what about his own constituency, his own beleaguered countrymen? Granted his talents at acquiring a devoted following, what if it had been to another end? Or, what if Mao had taken to his Yenan cave for spiritual not revolutionary reasons and emerged to preach personal enlightenment as the goal? Would his flock not have ended up the same as these, and China still as wretched as the workers in their hovels over here?

Bhagwan hates Mao. I don't think I'll ask him about that.

A little orange boy who'd gone to sleep is now before him. "What do you think about Maharishi?" he asks, and everybody finds this side-splitting, no doubt because they'd have liked to ask it themselves. "You are dangerous!" says Bhagwan. "A good man, Maharishi, a very good man, but whatsoever he is doing is very ordinary. You ask great questions!" The boy gives him a painting and returns to his snooze. It is my turn.

A chat about how things are going: I tell him how well I feel, that his prescription seemed to work. "Very good," he replies, then more sharply: "Now why are you waiting for sannyas?"

I supply my reservations as I'd thought about them earlier, referring to my father, "who is a very religious man and who always taught me to listen to what Christ had *said*, rather than to what any church had made of him. I find your wisdom accessible to me as coming from a human, but not if it's divine. And the mala and the orange are like a crucifix or an icon to me . . ."

"Then wait," he interrupts, not without irritation.

". . . But I am with you in my heart completely . . ."

"You cannot be!" he says, recoiling perceptibly. "Otherwise these complications cannot be there. They cannot be there!"

It's chilly out here in this hot night. Another try: "Well, I feel to the extent of my own limits that I am."

"Then wait," he repeats. Calming down. Door ajar. "Soon you will go beyond your limits, mm? And if you really understand Jesus, you will understand me immediately. And if you cannot see divine wisdom in me, you cannot see it in Jesus either, because it is a question of vision."

Tilt. It is so unfair, to misconstrue my point this way; I feel frustrated as a child confronted by authority for an unknown sin. But protocol appears to deny anyone but him the right to interrupt, and on he goes.

"It is not a question of where you can see and where you cannot see it. If you can see, you will see it in Buddha and Jesus and in Mohammed. And sometimes you will be able to see it in a small child, because the human and the divine are not divided. The human is divine."

"I agree" (of course I agree; he is not answering me), "but to put something on a pedestal takes it out of my reach and out of my possibilities."

"You just wait." He waggles his finger. "I will make your possibilities bigger. Just wait. One has to go beyond the limits—only then one grows. If you remain within your limits, you will never grow. One has to adventure a little beyond one's possibilities. One has to move into the unknown, the unfamiliar. Remain close to your boundary but go a little beyond. But if you remain confined to the boundary, you cannot grow. But wait . . . it is coming. It will come. When are you leaving?"

"I have to leave in two days."

"Think about sannyas before you leave. It is coming. It

will be difficult for you to leave without sannyas!" He is smiling, but his voice isn't.

Ma Deva Yama is in full flow outside. She has to register her new name at the office, then has invited me to join her celebration at a restaurant in town. We meet two orange friends of hers and the three of them make me feel like the mother of a newly stillborn child at someone else's christening. I am rejected and misunderstood—and stupid, not being able to convey such a simple idea as mine seems to be; while the others, who are as laughing, crying, feeling, as *there* as Yama-Fiorenza herself, treat me with a studied compassion that makes the freeze more solid than ever. How have I been maneuvered into this position of defensiveness? In this totalitarian, conformist world I ought to be used to it by now, to the nonperson treatment, at least without despair. I only want to be an honest witness, a seeker forever, sannyasin never. But after so many years of staying on the outside, and having to fight to be there when fights don't even come into it, I'm getting awfully tired.

August 16

Before last night's darshan I submitted a good question for this morning's discourse: "Why do you let people call you God? What does God call you?" However, Bhagwan not only ignores the question—for the first time he never looks at me, conveying a personal anger that rationally I know cannot be there. In that case who is angry with me?

Bhagwan is. Suddenly to illustrate a point in someone else's question he is saying, "Last night a dogmatic Christian came to see me . . ." and I cannot doubt that I am meant, although bemused at how my words got so distorted. I want a right of appeal! Now with this public condemnation it's as though the whole place is turning on me—no doubt as imaginary a sensation as his anger—while I am safely labeled hopeless. I may be hopeless, but a dogmatic Christian?

"Being here with me is an act of love. I have nothing else to give you except my love. I have nothing else to share with you except my love. While you are here with me . . . you will feel that you have been with me and that you have not been with me. Both are true, and both are true together. That's the paradox of love."

This really is a love affair with all things said that love refrains from speaking, or expresses in another way. That's the paradox of Bhagwan—he must concretize with words, for lack of other tools, the feelings he would advocate one merely feel. I think of youthful seductions in the backs of cars.

"If you are here for a longer period—and the period is not as important as the depth of the relationship. . . . That is the meaning of sannyas—it is a plunge into a deeper intimacy, into a deeper commitment."

Come on, you can't stay a child forever. Live. It won't hurt. I promise.

"Just the other night a woman was asking, 'If I don't take sannyas, will you accept me?' I told her, 'Yes, I accept you—whether you take sannyas or not is irrelevant—but *you* will not be able to accept *me* if you don't take sannyas.' "

Of course I love you unconditionally, but you can hardly

expect me to believe that you love me. You're just a tease.

"If you are able to accept me, then sannyas is just a gesture of your acceptance, nothing else."

Why are you making such a big deal? Everybody does it.

"It is just a gesture that you are coming with me, that you are ready to be with me . . . that even if I am going to hell you are coming with me; you would rather be in hell with me than in heaven alone, that's all. I'm not promising you that I will take you to heaven; nothing of the sort. Maybe I am going to hell."

It's all right, honey, I've got everything taken care of. If you get pregnant I might even marry you.

"A sannyasin is one who has trusted me; who says: 'Okay, so I am coming with you.' "

If you really love me as you say, prove it.

"Then something starts transpiring between me and you. It is not only changing your clothes, it is not only changing your name. It is simply dropping your whole past and starting from a-b-c."

My dearest virgin bride, let me make you over in my image.

"That's why I give you a new name—just to give you a new start, as if you are born again."

Mrs. John Smith. (You fell for it before; what stops you now?)

Pankaja goes shopping with me. We talk about a London friend of ours who's taken sannyas but not too seriously (am I trying to think up outs to be in?) and Pankaja attributes it to "too much ego." I ask her, beyond knowing, if she thinks that's my problem too. The rickshaw is bumping about so badly we can barely hold on to it and our packages, and the question is easier without having to look her in the eye. Her reply is elliptical in any case: "Some people have to get some before they can drop it." If that's applicable to me, I'm hardly likely "to get some" in this atmosphere. What about the matter of Christian dogmatism? This is harder. Since he can't be wrong, there's got to be something in it. I do come from a long line of Church of England clerics. Is it in the genes? They're a bit far back for me to be accused of their particular species of dogmatism, if any, but perhaps there's some dogmatic *reaction* going on. So go her more far-fetched speculations. I still feel misrepresented, misinterpreted, and miserable.

Most of all about our friendship. I came out here to chase its future, pursue the promise of continued camaraderie, loyalty forever, linked arms in the sunset, the gang of three. What preposterous illusions! It is used and done, the way it was. I cannot reinvent it or impose my dream on them. They have their own. They're finished with what was. I never finish anything. That's my problem. And, desperately flailing about for a last illusion, entertain the thought: *Maybe if I could just go through with it . . .*

Spend the afternoon in distress with Mulk in a local museum, where a frail old man exhibits his personal collection of betel-nut cutters. Mulk understands my account of the darshan business, but he (together with the sound of my vain rationalizations) makes me feel like a coward for not taking this visit to its potential consummation. No sooner have I said to Mulk, "It's not a possibility for me, becoming orange," than I hear the echo of Bhagwan's voice: "One must adventure beyond one's possibilities." How ridiculous! What does he know? On the other hand, without doing it, what do I know? How *will* I find out if there is something else? I've always tried to say Yes, and haven't a regret in all my life except the times I went away from an experience. Perhaps it's like giving birth: painful when you fight and glory when you welcome it and only give. *I can't say no and hope to understand.* (Saying yes is no guarantee either.) Help!

Arriving back at the ashram I make an appointment for

another darshan tomorrow, my final night. That way I can do it. I want to do it. Why not? Why not suspend my disbelief, what's left of it? It can't be any worse than this. "All pain comes from resistance" is Dinah's version of a Bhagwan motto; and it occurs to me that I am spending too much energy resisting social pressure when, long after these people have blurred into one, there may be that other problem: regret. I have reached the point where I can't bear *not* to do it—if only for fear of all the "What ifs . . ." that may trail me forever. Besides, I'm feverishly curious to know my name, and what it represents, and to hear some final words. If taking sannyas is the only way to see him again before I leave, then even that is worth it. I'm also conscious that my reasoning is about as mad as that which brought me to consent to the most inauspicious seduction; but isn't he always saying he doesn't mind about reasons?

At the same time I'm very angry to have been driven to these lengths—and not even sorry, on that account, that my motives are questionable. He's *not* interested in motives. "Make the leap." If, after all, he demands instant allegiance and is ready to call someone sannyasin who has not qualified with a year's wandering as a saddhu with a begging bowl—as any true sannyasin must have done—then he deserves all the second thoughts and backtracking he surely gets.

All right, let's make this bloody leap then! My whole life is made of leaps. Why perversely refuse the one leap that's called one? What harm will it do anyone? Only my self-esteem in London will suffer, and if you act for the sake of other people's opinions you might as well be living in a play, not a life. Let's just see if I can do it. Watch, says Bhagwan. I am going to watch me do it. Watch with an inner eye, as that may be the only one available. Part of me is definitely not looking. I remember being dared a score of times to ride a roller-coaster and it was just as awful the last time as the first. I did it, but I kept my eyes closed.

But how *will* I face people if I go home orange? How will I tell them who Bhagwan is? Words lose him: repeated, they are dead. The more fully made flesh he is, the more ephemeral he becomes. I am almost able to take seriously the idea that he is just a mouthpiece, the reed the wind blows through—because try as I do, I can produce no satisfactory description of him. I can say he is like velvet, Zen, a sunrise. (What Bagwash.) And he has astonishing capacities for finding wisdom in his daily talks (and losing it). And a concentration so absolute on what is there that he envelops it and moves inside it (except when he misses entirely). But who is he? Who is he? His own attempts to explain only justify his protestations about the impossibility of explaining. They are not just pompous and crazy, but misleading because they reveal nothing. His grandfather died beside him on an oxcart when he was seven, and he took to trusting no relationships. So? Why didn't he become a snake charmer or a Sri Avinashilingam? He fell out of a tree when he was twenty-one and got enlightened. It's better than a concussion. His last life was seven hundred years ago and he had to arrange to die prematurely (provoking a murder) since that's the only way you get to be reborn. What does anyone know about seven hundred years ago or this ingenious strategy of return? He was hanging around all these eons looking for the right time, the right parents. Surely one can bring no more to such implausible claims than belief, or its lack. It's like Devopama inviting me to join a chain letter and when I declined (on the grounds that it doesn't work) replying, "But it's quite a sannyasin trip, really. If you have *faith* in it, it works."—and I have faith in nothing. People to whom I'll mention Bhagwan will still react hysterically out of their most negative or positive extremes, as if it's got to be a matter of faith, to be clung to or denounced. I can't expect to find much interest simply in the phenomenon of this man, whom anybody would have to agree is Somebody.

The point about being Somebody is to be rewarded with *attention*. Attention is the most valuable of human commodities to be bestowed on one. It is the *sine qua non* of love. If you are famous, rich, or powerful, people never forget meeting you or your name or your face; indeed they see more in you than is even there, they are paying so much attention. But to encounter Somebody who goes further and claims to be Nobody and God at once; Somebody with whom the subject of attention is the entire message; and Somebody capable of inspiring the vast exertions forced on visitors to Poona—from the acquisition of a ticket to India, through all the petty indignities devised as "tests," to the final confrontation with those eyes—is to deal with rather an extraordinary presence. One gives this man willy-nilly the most minutely detailed attention, if only to justify the insane investment. When he is then able to show remarkable perceptiveness it is hardly surprising. Not only is he gifted with the quality of attention himself but the same is returned to him so fully that he has quite a lot to go on. Sitting at his feet is to quiver with life, to be thoroughly involved, to be exposed to the light with lens wide. One must trust him not to abuse what is shown him because to distrust him in any substantive way means to distrust oneself.

Compare meeting Bhagwan with meeting another middleaged Indian, Clara. Having heard about Clara I was aware that she was not uninteresting, that she would be a convenience for me, that it was of some importance to be on decent terms with her. But for days her name eluded me despite the fact that it was the only Western—therefore memorable—name I heard. I am not *aware* of her, except negatively; if the food isn't there or doesn't suit me or the bathroom is muddy again or I can't find my clothes. She in turn wants tips from me and does what she thinks might earn them, no more no less. If you ask her about me next year she may just recall my unusually blue clothes in all the orange she must wash. I show her nothing else. As for me, I'll have to think hard to remember her face. I never bothered to learn much about her, and will forget even that. Yet there is nothing I wouldn't like to know about Bhagwan, down to the most mundane detail. He is simply riveting, if only because he has riveted so many others and that alone is of interest. He is the centerpiece of an elaborate banquet table, and he is the dinner too, the wine and speaker all in one. Clara is a waitress. He is the main item in the consciousness of many thousands of people. Clara's family cares about her and her employers do as well when she doesn't turn up. These are the regrettable facts. Since most of us are like Clara and so few are like Bhagwan, we should all, ego-schmego, be interested in how he does it.

The sense of inadequacy bred by the realization that one is just a Clara of this world is overcome, however, if one can attribute special powers to Bhagwan. To raise his level with worship is like raising the water in a lock: You can't expect *me* to swim up there. The fact that he disavows this, insisting on the divinity of us all, is unassimilable as it is and simply introduces the need for another category altogether. He may not be holier-than-thou, but he's *some*thinger-than-thou. What? He will tell you. He is enlightened, a living master. Well then *that* is God. Whatever you call it (X, Y, Z), his followers will treat it as God, as a being superior to themselves (or why follow him?), and what else is God but man's perfected self-image? He is there to show you that it's possible—and why shouldn't it be if so many believe and confirm it in their daily reactions to him? He must have worked very hard to get where he is today, but it is a place out of reach for most, a place from which it is rather easier to be divine than from Clara's rocky well among the dirty clothes. He is on a chair on a platform; we are on the floor. We never stand when he stands; we do not even know how tall he is, as another's height relative to a squatting person is not measurable without trigonometry. He is indulged in every way. Being the object of the passionate love of many imaginative people, the quality of the indulgence is amazing. He is capable of accepting that love; that is his supreme difference. Most people can't handle unqualified adoration, even from only one other person, believing themselves unworthy of it. *He believes himself worthy of it.*

The lesson of Bhagwan is that you are as important as you feel. If you can feel the God in you as he does, then you are God. It would be unusual if Clara felt herself to be God—an Indian female is unlikely to have had the chance to get the hang of it. And what would such a God do with her seven children? Give them inspiration for dinner? Of course it would help to be treated as Bhagwan is treated, but even beyond existing in his divinely privileged life she would have to have earned it with an equivalently divine and articulate confidence. The rest of us call such confidence a manifestation of ego. If getting thousands of people to declare their allegiance to you by prominently wearing a picture of your face isn't an expression of ego, then what is it?

But he says he has no ego. Then *ego*, like *God*, is a word requiring another definition. And if I could put together all these confusions then I would be a Bhagwan not a Clara. In the meantime all I can do is bask in his words, the tantalizing taste of God in them. You could call the lectures God lessons, and you could describe Bhagwan's efforts as trying to make us all feel worthy of them—while he succumbs gracefully to the worship which contradicts their content. So what? "I am full of contradictions," he says.

Savita says she dreamed of Bhagwan before she had ever thought of coming to India. "He was a Chinaman in a barn, dressed in rags, and all he said to me was 'Seven Years.' "

"How did you know he was Bhagwan?"

She shrugs. "I knew. Miracles keep happening to me like that."

It seems that last week, fed up with all of us one morning, she took herself off after the dynamic to the Blue Diamond for breakfast. "I was very confused, and thinking there is only one person in the world I can speak to now, but I don't even think she's *here*." This person was an encounter group leader whom she'd known in London two years ago and who, she subsequently heard, had come to India. But when she'd written from London to Poona several months ago she had no response, and assumed the group leader had moved on. "But do you know, she was at the next table at the Blue Diamond! She leaned over to borrow the salt! Then she recognized me and said hello, and I asked her, 'Did you get my letter?' and—do you know what she said? She said 'Yes, but I gave it to Bhagwan and he told me not to worry about it because you were coming.' Really amazing, that."

I'm getting mixed up. "You mean, his saying you were coming?"

"Yes, because the extraordinary thing is that I hadn't even *thought* of coming when I wrote."

Clara, perhaps in gratitude for some extra funds we donated after she'd pawned her necklace in a demonstration of dire need, has made us a feast for dinner, and afterward we stay in atypical peace around the table. The single German who can still put up with our contingent starts a Mozart tape, makes order, and lights candles. Savita has a stomachache; Devopama lays her out on the couch and waves a lit stick of incense over the offending part in one of his arcane healing procedures. Pankaja flattens herself on the floor with closed eyes, meditating to the music. I have found my own meditation: watching two chameleons engaged in a patient hunt for cockroaches. Poised on the wall whose off-white color it's assumed, moving nothing but the occasional eye, one lizard outwaits an entire sonata, ever alert and undistracted by the tiny flies that flick at the light. Before I've even seen the roach it's gone, in a single cinematic frame. The other chameleon, waiting on the curtain and purplish to match, darts out now for its turn at what must be the prime spot. They exchange places. Neat. Tomorrow is my birthday, my turn. Will it make the slightest difference, approached this way? What a dismal situation. What made me ever think I had free will? Can I get out of here before I sell my soul? As well might the roach escape the lizard's tongue.

I hear Bhagwan's voice saying quite clearly, "Why are you worrying about the future? It will hap-pen."

August 17

An innovation for the discourse: They have started to have people stand on line. People join at dawn, taking turns to fetch some tea or breakfast. This takes care of one of the last bits of day which was heretofore unstructured. It also institutionalizes the superior status of the ashram residents, as there are *two* lines, and the ashram line, although it does not begin to form until a short time before the discourse, files in before the hoi polloi.

Pankaja and I wait with the latter as she talks of joining the former. So many people are backed up in the wait for a room in the ashram, and no new ones are ready. She has not only applied but donated five thousand dollars; Laxmi keeps promising, but it's delayed until another building is completed. What will she do here then? "Whatever he says." How about writing? Her journal is nearly finished, according to his direction, and that is that. "I don't need to write any more."

"But what if we need you to write?" I ask. She shrugs.

The line edges in. I have waited an hour, and end up sitting where I sat yesterday without waiting at all. Pankaja stations herself at the side as always, where she can find a bit of wall to lean on for her backache.

This morning's lecture is an outrage. He's got dogmatic Christians on his mind again, not to mention dogmatic Christians' fathers, and the whole package seems to suggest to him a fierce paternal tyranny—Schreber!—the nineteenth-century German Dr. Spock who thought to purify the race by snuffing out disobedience in the cradle. The inventor of special sleeping and sitting harnesses to pinion his and other people's children, Schreber advocated the destruction of the will before it could attempt (at a theoretical six months) to exert itself. Bhagwan's moral is to be yourself, find your own destiny, drop the "conscience" of others and obey your own (spend an hour at night tracing back your thoughts to source so you can drop them). You can only do what *you* were meant to do, not what your parents made you do.

He is definitely looking at me this morning. A continuation of yesterday's hallucination, no doubt, but I am receiving this message: He has decided to forgive me by seeking out the causes of my waywardness, and has conjured up this Schreber business for an explanation. Did he just go deaf the other night after I spoke the word *father*? Are strong fathers really the threat here? Can't take the competition, eh? Can't he visualize a father who is strong and not tyrannical? Assuming any of this to be so, he is telling me to exchange my fiendish harnessing father for a kind, forgiving one, to wit himself. (Interpreted the other way, of course, "Be yourself" is just as easily interpreted as "Don't take sannyas if it's against yourself": But since he never says that, one can safely conclude he isn't saying it now.) In the end, it's his effort that moves me; why is he going out on such a limb? If I am succumbing to the seduction not through passion but compassion, I'm succumbing nonetheless.

Have to hang around the house again packing to leave tomorrow and washing my hair. People are getting used to me wet, but nobody's ever heard of so many darshans in a row. One of our Germans has been trying to get in for weeks, but after finally achieving the coveted appointment she caught a cold and had to wait "to let the body recover." To expedite a cure she took a course of an Ayurvedic remedy which, while having the desired effect on the cold (eventually), left her with some sort of lingering odor, and rejection at the gates has now become a habit.

Stray conversation overheard between trips to the bathroom. An argument about Maharaj Ji—one faction insisting he's a spurious master and another that he's been enlightened since birth—is settled to everyone's satisfaction but mine by the comment, "It doesn't matter anyway. It's good for you to worship someone." And talk about the groups: the way Bhagwan assigns people to this one or that as he thinks it remedial for this or that condition. For some reason ashram residents are exempt from these, as also from the meditations. They exchange tips about the Tath-ata, which is partly "secret" in that you are not supposed to be prepared for the initial challenge: "Tell the group something about yourself you have never revealed before." (I can't think of anything I've never revealed before, but as a game it sustains my interest through two shampoos.) Then there is a call for a display of "*real* anger, *real* sex-uality." (Since the inspiration for this sex or anger will be neither love nor frustration but the incitement of a leader, it is hard to see how it is very *real*.) The source of this information, an American who's dropped by, demonstrates part of what is meant by showing off various bruises on his arms and thighs. "I really got into my aggression," he marvels. It's his turn to listen then to what's in store for him at the Enlightenment Intensive he's starting next week. He will be asked by an assigned interlocutor "Who are you?" over and over and over; then they exchange places and he will do the asking instead. This goes on for several *days*, and in answering you must not repeat yourself. Listen-ing to your accessory becomes the tedious part, it is reported; the tendency is for the questioner to doze off and need a prod to ask you who you are again. Sounds like a good old-fashioned London cocktail party to me, only with nothing to drink.

I brought just one orange dress to India and it doesn't cover enough of me for mosquito protection, so I must bor-row Pankaja's flowing ochre darshan outfit. What am I going to do about being orange? I know I'll not throw out my clothes. And wear a mala? Savita is furious with hers, its weight and ugliness, and flings it around her head like a ball and chain. Pankaja has a pretty one, old style, that went out more than a year ago and confers on its wearers the special cachet of being a bit more equal than others. (Owners of such reliquaries exchange addresses of local silversmiths who will make pretty borders for eleven "rupes." The newer model comes prebordered in thick wood.) Savita is trying to adjust to the idea, passed on by a sannyasin of a year's standing, that while "the orange and the mala don't stop grating on you, they are supposed to—they are irritants specifically to keep you reminded." But she can't imagine what to tell her patients. And I my daughter?—"But you *promised.*" Well, I'll drop it if she's offended. What do I care about any of this compared to my children? I'd rather be a hypocrite to Bhagwan than to Eve.

Pankaja and Savita are so pleased with my progress that they're almost willing to make peace over it. Savita is still somewhat astonished that I've joined her, but Pankaja exudes a horrible complacency suggesting she never had a doubt. What was that question so long ago in London about feeling manipulated? It's a peculiar sensation, giving in after all that resistance. I have forgotten why I bothered. People I met on their arrival who most violently insisted that they weren't getting involved have, without a single exception, appeared soon after in purest orange, looking at me more or less sheepishly, depending on the extent of their initial opposition. Sheepish, all right. Baa-a-a.

It's a curious darshan tonight. Because of laxity at the last one—suspected smellies let into the presence anyway, if scarved—Bhagwan sniffed out something potentially fatal to his body and decreed a renewed stringency. As a result hardly anybody passes, and only seven of us eventually file in. Even he looks surprised at how few there are.

I am called. "Oh, *you!*" he says, grinning with what almost seems to be affection. Or is it the same complacency I saw in Dinah? There is not the slightest question anymore that I was doomed to end up here. "Are you ready?" Nod. "Close your eyes."

For a long time I sit before him as if encapsulated, with only the scratching of the master's pen and the flash of Shiva's camera through my lids to remind me what a pretty pass I've come to. It's all quite funny really. Mostly I feel that I've been here before. He is right, recommending the impulsive jump. How much easier to have done it like Fiorenza and Karen, and spared myself all that confusion. But it also means something to be recognized, if only as a troublemaker, and ego notwithstanding. With sixty thousand sannyasins, how does he know who they all are? And if I had materialized pre-oranged out of the blue, I'd never have been able to suspend my suspicions that the name was arbitrary, unconnected to me.

"Right." I open my eyes as he puts on the mala, touching it and my head for a moment. "This will be your name: Ma Deva Kanan. Can you pronounce it?" I say it after him, KAHnahn. "Deva means divine and kanan means a wild forest: Divine Wild Forest." He shows me the paper on which he has inscribed it in English and Sanskrit, together with his fanciful curlicued signature. His smile engulfs me. "That's what you have to keep in your heart—that to be wild is to be alive. The more civilized a person is, the less alive. I'm not saying to become uncivilized. I'm not saying to break the rules and regulations of the society, but remember deep inside that all the rules and regulations, and the civilization and the society, are a game. Never lose contact with your inner wilderness [wild-erness, he says]. When you close your eyes, just become wild. When you are alone in your room, just become wild. Sing and dance and do things without any consideration of others.

"A person who is continuously considering others, never grows. When you are moving with people in the world, consider them, but remember that these rules are not commandments. They have nothing to do with truth. They are just conveniences. Of course one has to take care on the road to keep to the left or keep to the right; it has to be so. But keeping to the left has no truth about it, no fundamental . . . no ultimacy about it. It is just a rule of the game. If you want to walk on the road, you have to follow the rule. But when you are in your room alone, meditating, then there is no need to continuously keep to the left. Then you can just run in the middle of the road. You can forget all that society imposes, forces. That's what is going to help your growth.

"And whenever you can find time, move into the forest. Go to the wild sea. Just watching will be beautiful. Swimming will be beautiful . . . surfing will be beautiful . . . going to the mountains will be beautiful. Keep more in touch with the nonhuman, and you will become capable of reaching to the superhuman. Don't be confined to the human.

"On both sides of the human, two worlds open. On one side is the world of the nonhuman—the trees, the birds, the rivers, the mountains, the stars; on the other side, the superhuman—the world of God. It is difficult to know right now about the world of God, but one way is that you can drop out of the human world. You can become part of the nonhuman existence. And that will give you the clue about how to go above the human. If you can go below, you can go above. The same key opens and functions both ways.

"Once you know that human boundaries can be crossed," he says, "then you know where those boundaries are and how to cross them. One becomes by and by efficient, more and more skillful.

"Do you have something to say now?" he asks suddenly, and I can only laugh. I have nothing to say. (*Surfing?*)

Back at the house people react to my mala as if they've never seen one before. Savita takes my new name as a justification for all the advice she's ever given me; the others are in a state of swoon at its poetry. I want to forego the obligatory celebration since the return trip beginning tomorrow will leave out two nights and I would rather sleep. Lying in bed waiting for Savita to return from the bathroom I make great efforts to stay awake so I can remind her to turn on the fan. It's too complicated to get up and do it myself as I've already swathed my bed in its mosquito netting, tucking it all in from inside. Gazing up at the soft, dirty-white billows, I amuse myself with the way some folds fall into the configuration of a face. It's a familiar face, but resists identification. Actually it's smiling at me, as the moon does when I'm feeling good, but taunting me, too, for my lack of recognition. Then I see that it is *my* face, exactly my face, and it is smiling not with mockery but with explosive joy. Fascinated, transfixed, I spy on myself, seeing the face not as if mirrored or photographed but wholly from some objective exterior point, and with color and contour and expressive life. As I watch, the colors fade. I think the apparition itself is fading, but the dimming is of another kind: the face growing old. It falls into wrinkles, the flesh in flaccid folds, the eyes gaze sadly into centers I have never seen, and the smile is slowly gone, until only a terrible sorrow is left. In the end I am isolated in this skin. I have no children, parents, friends or Gods—there's only me, alone to die. And yet—I have created this universe, and it's enough. I'll go ahead with it.

From a curious interest, my state turns to fear, then awe. By the time Savita returns I can't move, afraid to blink lest it go, yet desperate for it to go. I start to tell her what I've seen, I have seen myself, I have seen—but with the first words the face truly starts to vanish, and searching will not bring it back, or even suggest where it had been, there is nothing but mosquito net. I remember to remind Savita about the fan.

Afterword

I sent this diary to Poona for Pankaja and Savita to read. Bhagwan saw it too and on April 27, 1980, commented in his discourse. Both Pankaja and Savita sent me a copy of the tape. "She escaped," he said. "Now she writes a book about the whole experience. And she says I don't know what happened—why I became a sannyasin. There is something which *pulls* you. There is something intangible; one cannot figure out what it is exactly, but something like hypnosis. Seen first, it may be in the eyes of Bhagwan or in the sound of his voice that one feels to become a sannyasin: even I became a sannyasin. But then I became very much afraid that now I am being pulled the same way in this orange whirlpool in which Pankaja has disappeared, Savita has disappeared. It is better before I am too much in it and escape becomes impossible, to escape. . . . Now, writing this book, she is trying to convince herself that she has done the right thing. She has done the most stupid thing of her life. . . . And the opportunity is still not lost, Kanan, wherever you are in the world: my eyes are reaching there too. And whatsoever I am saying here, the sound of my voice goes on resounding around the earth. If you have even a little bit of intelligence you will be pulled back into the orange whirlpool."

Who knows? It seems inconceivable, but going to the ashram in the first place was not high among probabilities, and all is in a constant state of change, as Bhagwan never tires of telling us. I am certainly less ready to dismiss anything, now I've had the experience of sitting at the (lovingly pedicured) toes of the Indian holy man. The signs of the sannyasin, however, went immediately—never in fact got started (except for Savita's sake, when she returned to London to tie off the ends of her life here, and said she couldn't talk to anyone who wasn't orange; but we couldn't really talk anyway). A few people used my new name, seriously or not, for a short time, then forgot about it. Bhagwan's advice stayed with me but wild forests and surfing are not exactly applicable to London life, unless you care to extract something metaphoric from them (with potentially far-fetched results).

There has been a lot of passionate anger among friends, going to show that irrationality is a democratically distributed trait. My children, with the clarity of vision Bhagwan so admires, are uniquely capable of sustained sanity when the subject of the guru comes up. "I don't think Bhagwan should tell people what to wear," Eve said. "I suppose it's to see if they really love him." Moby commented after a visit to the London Rajneesh Centre: "Don't ask me what, but those people are leaving something out." After my return from India I used to play cassettes of the daily discourses in the car. The children made me turn it off. There wasn't any point in arguing with them that I found much of value in Bhagwan's miscellany of wisdom. Maybe he doesn't say a lot that they don't know anyway. A great deal of it has the quality, indeed, of something found again, recognizable for having been known before and for some reason forgotten. I am very grateful to Bhagwan for reminding me. Gratitude I owe him; fealty, not. The sycophancy and paranoia in his followers, all the gimmicks of power that seduce initiates and secure their submission—group pressure, bullying, isolation, the Us versus Them outlook—seem to have influenced him as well. If he were more interested in the truth behind his words than in the sound of his voice proclaiming them, he could not say I had "escaped." It is disappointing, in fact, that the many sources he has culled and the effective synthesis he has made of them are submerged by a banal organization which counts heads over blessings. But if I am happy at home with my children, does wearing orange prove it? Yet I am happier since Poona, largely because of what I learned through Bhagwan.

This is neither complicated nor original: I had just been looking in the wrong direction for too long, without attention too often. Acting consciously, absorbing yourself entirely in what you do, can make moments that were merely survived, habitual and dull, into extraordinary occasions for joy. I knew this already but used it with reserve, in compartments. The surrender is not to a man or a belief but back to something in oneself. To see that was to change not at all and yet entirely. Whether he made me see it or whether living through the event stripped the layers off doesn't matter. I'm content to give him credit: He was there.

"But what *use* is happiness?" asked a friend who described herself as "too linear" for this sort of thing. "Does it help you get things done?" To such a question I don't know what to say, since I can't repeat the pre-Poona injunction that provoked the homicidal in me: "I used to feel that way too." All my life I have been working for tomorrow; and if tomorrow was going to be better, reflections on today were necessarily unfavorable. I have a much altered way of looking at now, now. However I would dispute Bhagwan's exclusion of all tenses but the present. There may be plenty to rejoice about in every moment; but there is also much in that moment involving the physical misery of millions whose future must be accounted for. In the long run (if there is a long run), Bill Pirie's work is more significant than Bhagwan's. The important thing is still for people to have enough to eat.

But there is nothing wrong, or even difficult, about joining the two. At any rate I cannot discard my conscience on the comfortable grounds that it is a manifestation of ego. But neither can I work for a just and pleasant future with the grimness many give "the struggle." The guilt which generates solemnity and prohibits joy achieves nothing. Dance, says Bhagwan. Why not? Why toil and struggle when you can dance to the same end? Because the way you approach a goal affects it: but what matters is to keep to the goal.

Bhagwan would probably not appreciate this picking and choosing, nor my strange view of him as a kind of life's handyman. But my quarrel with him, never resolved, persists: that his value recedes as he claims superhumanity. He has helped me to see the God in myself and in others, but I can't see in him any more than in the rest of us. Attention may resemble, but is not, love. He is not a saint or a prophet. The humility is missing. The contradiction between his movement and its Indian setting, the orange, well-fed view which disguises the reality of such intolerable poverty, must make one dispute his pretensions to Buddhahood or Christliness. Would Buddha carry an Yves Saint Laurent towel over his arm? Or Christ allow his disciples to turn out beggars?

The people in the ashram are, relative to their surroundings, even more than they have always been, society's rootless privileged. How easy to renounce what you've only felt guilty about anyway, especially when you can have it back any time. But what is their ideal vision of the world—

everybody meditating, still, aware? Is work still needed?
Who does it? This implies castes, Brahmans on down. What
is new in that? It's just a system of oppression like the ideologies it discards. Otherwise, such a mode of life is only possible for a parasitical elite subsidized by money from outside.

In the final analysis, however, I failed Bhagwan more than
the other way around. If I had wanted a guru, I might well
have found one in him. Ruth Prawer Jhabvala, talking on
the BBC on the subject of gurus, said: "I'd like to take it
seriously, but unfortunately I've never met anybody I could
take wholly seriously. . . . And then the disciples are enough
to bring anybody down." I agree; yet one has to take seriously the *phenomenon* of disciples and gurus, and their
proliferation now. It is a historical event of importance to
the West. Wishing it to disappear won't make it. Wounded
by the world which bred them, people rush to give themselves away to—as a British journalist recently wrote—"the
many pseudo-religious cults which . . . are, to put it at its
lowest, sinister and dangerous." Anyone who can get away
with imposing his power on others appears to have no
trouble finding them. We bring up our children to submit
to concentric circles of authority and in the end they can't
do without it. In the view of many of them, life is empty
in this empty, finished world. We are socially dependent,
but when the links are broken it becomes a question of
listening to the most beguiling voice, whatever it says.
Heroes are hard to come by. Worldly leaders with messages
of hope soon grow corrupt or are gunned down. Give us
God! And here are teachers—more or less "sinister and dangerous" (and all of them false except Bhagwan, according to
Bhagwan)—who answer that the power itself is within *you*:
maybe the last reliable source left.

But the God of the self is a despotic God, and there is an
irony in becoming enslaved to a search for what is actually

free. Ultimately this search can so obscure the vision that nothing remains but the self—or that part of it which is left after suspending the critical faculty and casting off history, morality, your own culture and the people you love. To give these up and call it nirvana is like cutting your arm off and proclaiming your health.

Such an extreme concentration on the self may explain what happened to our friendship, Dinah's and Judith's and mine. The two who have stayed in Poona are no longer friends; but to some extent their love had turned to hostility as long ago as their interest in Bhagwan began. When I got involved there was further disintegration. It is hard to see from a diary of those days how fond we once were of each other, and harder to find the "religion" in feelings which atomize love. Hardest of all is to identify in my friends a God who makes them lose their intense concern for others. I miss the three of us laughing together, but I miss more the brave Dinah who went to Vietnam and the soft-hearted Judith who cried when she saw the beggars of Bombay.

"You didn't understand anything," Savita writes to me. Maybe I didn't, but I still worry about questions which are not addressed in Poona, so our correspondence is unilluminating. It is very limited at the best of times. I hear about them, of course. I am insatiably curious about who they have become—these people whom I loved and thought I knew—but letters do no good. In common with other members of the ashram, their disbelief in the Indian post makes them scribble hurried notes for departing sannyasins to mail abroad. This allows no time except for a brief message of affection, with a description of the bliss attending them as they write, the iridescence of a sunbeam in a cobweb or the particular look of the moon: very here-now. No mention of the past, either recent or distant, or reflection or analysis, let alone news of each other.

They have little contact. Savita has become very high up in the ashram. A recent visitor said "She walks like a duchess. She hasn't changed at all." I had already heard from Polly, our once revolutionary friend who is now a permanent Poona resident too, that Bhagwan gave up personal conversations when the huge numbers ruled them out, and instead holds a nightly "energy darshan" in which Savita plays a key role. He touches both a "medium" and the kneeling supplicant on their third eyes, while the medium embraces the head of the kneeler, completing the circle of energy. Vivek, Bhagwan's "shakti," is the medium sometimes, and sometimes it is Savita. This activity depletes her terribly, reported her mother—having visited Poona distressed, and returning in orange herself—and showed me a photograph of a Judith I never knew, hands clasped round a forehead with the great one's fingers in the appropriate places, her eyes rolled back, an abandon in her passion that indeed must take it out of her.

Pankaja was reported to have grumbled that she can never see Bhagwan anymore without Savita being there. For a long time, while Savita edited the darshan books, had access to Bhagwan's amazing library and lived in the inner sanctum, Pankaja's job was to clean Savita's lavatory. Although you're meant to clean lavatories until you like it, I don't know if Pankaja got to like cleaning Savita's. In any case she was recently relieved of this duty and assigned to the Rajneesh theatrical company, which performs Shakespeare in orange costumes.

They are both committed to Bhagwan for good. Other considerations don't come into it. When I wrote to Pankaja complaining angrily on behalf of her children, both she and Savita answered the letter praising its "energy." Pankaja visited the children but wrote to them afterward that she had cried for three days, and wouldn't be coming again because it was "too painful." What was, seeing them or not seeing them?

Having begun in a state of extreme intolerance, I still have great sympathy for those who feel that the whole matter of guru-worship is diversionary, destructive, and boring. But when people react to Bhagwan as a threat to their rational existence, I would rather say that you get from him what you can take. You can ignore or discredit him, use what is illuminating in his words, have a good laugh, or give your life. Whatever the decision, it's yours and yours alone.